GREG CHAPMAN'S

CONDENSED HISTORIES

VOLUME 1

HISTORIES FROM ENGLAND

Published by Greg Chapman

Isle Of Wight, UK

ISBN 978-1-291-27134-8

There are so many people to thank and dedicate my work to, and I hope I have enough books to thank them all.

This first book I would like to dedicate to my parents and brothers – for everything.

Also to my dogs, and especially Shazu, my constant companion through the writing of this book.

Contents

Introduction ....- 7 -

Boudicca...- 10 -

Seahenge..- 17 -

Princes in the Tower ....- 22 -

Howard Carter...- 34 -

Origins of the English Civil War ....- 41 -

The Blitz Spirit ....- 47 -

Isabella de Fortibus ....- 52 -

The Magna Carta ....- 57 -

Jack the Ripper ....- 62 -

The Hundred Years War ....- 69 -

Charles Darwin ....- 75 -

Elizabethan Witches..- 81 -

Music Hall and Variety ....- 88 -

1066 ....- 93 -

The British Empire ....- 97 -

Final Thoughts...- 102 -

Introduction

I consider my relationship to history to be much the same as my relationship to foreign countries. I'm not saying here that I think that the past is like another country, as has famously been said before, as I have certain issues with that statement. I am talking specifically about my relationship with history. I like to travel, to see as much of the world as I can in my life, and hope to see more through this series of books. This means that most countries I pass through quickly, and stay in for only a short period. I will never truly get to know a country as well as I know my own, or even as well as I have come to know my second home country of Italy.

While most historical scholars have a 'home' subject or period in which they are experts, I like to think of myself as a traveller in history. I want to know a bit about everything that interests me in history, and I have never managed to tie myself down to a favourite period, era or subject. As such I will always have a passing knowledge of a range of different periods and subjects instead of a complete understanding of any one. In other words when it comes to history I consider myself to be a 'Jack of all trades, master of none'.

There are a lot of jokes and comments made among a certain section of the 'academic elite' in any field about those people who try to create a 'popular' version. To try and take writing about the subject out of the high realm of academia and to make it accessible to everybody.

From Tony Robinson, who does a wonderful job presenting 'Time Team' although he is not actually himself a trained archaeologist to the best of my knowledge (although he has spent a lot more time on digs than many who have trained in the field I would guess) to any television or film adaptation of Charles Dickens, Jane Austen, or Thomas Hardy, where literature snobs sit there and moan that they are not a patch on the original book. With books, a lot of the time I would have to agree that they are not as good as the originals. Not necessarily with Thomas Hardy's works, mind you, as I have never actually finished any of his books - although I did watch the recent TV adaptation of Tess of the D'Urbervilles with Gemma Arterton – but mainly because of her rather than for any reasons of plot!

I haven't yet read most of Dickens (although I have read a few and love them, and will read the rest one day), but I've seen a lot of the adaptations. I have read some Austen, and I have seen Pride and Prejudice, and I would say the book was better. It was more in depth. The film offers a window to the book, it can't contain it all.

When I watch Tony Robinson on 'Time Team' I enjoy watching it, it is a glimpse at history, at archaeology. They can't show too much in an hour long programme, nor is it their intention to do so. Sometimes after an episode I have become interested enough by a topic to go to the library or an online bookstore and get a book that covers it in more depth, sometimes I am just entertained by the little piece of history I have been given.

If you do not like bite-sized, non-academic chunks of history, intended to entertain and sometimes inspire further investigation, you will not like this book very much. The same as if you do not like watching adaptations of books you will never enjoy 'The Lord Of The Rings' trilogy however epic it was, because it cannot live up to the books!

Even at epic length though, in the super-advanced-blue-ray-extended-whatever-it-is-cut, the whole trilogy runs at about 12 hours. Whereas a quick look at the audio book tells me that 'The Fellowship of the Ring' alone is about twenty hours of reading time! It is so long since I last read the books I couldn't say for sure how this compares, because at the moment I don't have 50-60 hours to set aside to read it again - with an ever growing pile of books on a shelf already waiting to be read that I haven't read once, and an even greater list of books in my mind that I intend to read one day, and subjects I want to study – and that's before I get to my actual 'day job' of writing shows, books and working on new pieces of escapology, performing and everything else.

None of us has time to study everything in detail, but that doesn't mean we're not interested in knowing a little bit about it.

And that was a very long winded way of introducing you to the idea behind my 'Condensed Histories', including to the idea that there will be a lot of long winded and off topic moments in this book. Each chapter in this book is about a historical subject that I found interesting enough to research in some detail, and yet I have presented to you just an introduction, a glimpse into the subject, and also an idea of what the subject means to me.

I hope you enjoy, I hope some of you are inspired to learn more about some of these subjects, and I hope that anyone who disparages this book because it is not the height of academia will be content in the knowledge that I couldn't care less. I am an entertainer and traveller writing about a subject that entertains and interests me, and hopefully sharing a little knowledge.

When choosing topics for this book I have gone for one or two obvious points in history and historical figures, but I have also tried to go for some more obscure people and places. I haven't, however, aimed to fit in all the most famous or most important points in English history – just those that interested me as I looked through to decide on topics.

If this book still seems too long to read, just wait for someone to make an adaptation for the telly!

Greg

Boudicca

Queen of the Iceni

It has been said time and time again that it is a man's world, although I for one have always been a bit suspicious of this statement ever since I realised that although there are still relatively few women in the top levels of business and government, that with a simple smile and by asking in a certain tone of voice, a woman can get me to do just about anything. Please note that I didn't include the word 'pretty', 'beautiful', or any more crass words to suggest the same. It really doesn't matter who the woman is, from the sweet old lady who asks for help with her shopping, to the young woman who needs help reaching something off of a high shelf[1]. We all know that men are suckers for a pretty face, and a lot of people tend to think that is where it stops; but I think we are hard wired to respond to smiles and instructions from all women. Or perhaps it is just me. Interestingly, judging from some observations I have made, it is a genetic impulse that can be overridden by the attachment of a small piece of gold around the third finger of the left hand.

Of course, there are some women throughout history who people have just had to listen to, like it or not, because of their power, personality, or, let's be honest, because they happen to be amazingly attractive. In fact very often the female figures who have made it into the history books have been strong and often quite tough, purely because these are the types of women who were able to rise to power and find themselves 'worthy' of comment by historians.

Of all the women in history, however, one of my very favourites is a young lady from Norfolk, whose name is... well

---

[1] Although I do often have difficulties with that one, not being a particularly tall man.

actually that is a bit of a contentious issue, and one which I'm sure will upset someone whatever I say. When I was in school I learned it as Boadicea, which at that point in time and from early 19th century was the most common way of referring to her – although apparently[2] this stems from a mistake in a translation in the late 1700s. The correct English version of her name would be Boudicca (alternatively spelled Boudica). Other variations that appear in different works include Bunduca and Bodiga.

I will be calling her Boudicca, partly because it is how I am familiar with referring to her now, partly because that is what she is called in my copy of Tacitus' Annals, but mostly because I like it better than the others and it's my book.

Boudicca was the wife of Prasutagus, King of the Iceni people[3], and she is most famous for rising up in revolt against the Romans after the death of her husband to protest the Roman's plundering her land, raping her daughters, and beating her.

She rode into battle in a chariot with blades coming out from the wheels[4], and caused a lot of trouble for the Romans before the rebellion was finally crushed. There is no denying that this story obviously proves that hell really does have no fury like a woman scorned!

The story really begins with an agreement made between Prasutagus and the Romans, in which Prasutagus (or Pras as he

---

[2] As a note to people who are looking for the facts, whenever I use the word 'apparently', you can take this as shorthand that I found the fact in a couple of locations and found it somewhat interesting, but I couldn't find a source that I thought was reputable enough for me to be happy. In other words it's probably something I only found on the internet.

[3] Who, despite having, in my opinion, a much weirder name, doesn't seem to have suffered as much of an identity crisis throughout history as his wife. Maybe it is a man's world!

[4] Alright, the blades are more legend than fact. She almost certainly didn't have them owing to the fact that histories of the battle don't mention all of the troops alongside her having their legs chopped off at the knees, plus it wasn't something Britons did in battle. But it is still a striking image!

wasn't known to his friends but which is easier to type) agreed that the Iceni tribe, which ruled in roughly the area that is now Norfolk, would become an ally of Rome. This was probably a good idea, whether or not he trusted the Romans, considering that otherwise the Romans would have had him killed, and taken the tribe under Roman rule rather than allowing them to theoretically remain independent. As part of this deal, however, when he died the rule of the tribe (or kingdom) would pass to a join leadership between his two daughters and the Roman Emperor (then Claudius, but by the time he died Nero had taken the helm).

Come 61AD[5] Pras died. Is that a bit blunt? I considered using a euphemism -that he kicked the bucket, or passed away - but frankly I couldn't see the point in being delicate about death at this point in the book. I'm going to break some sad news to you now – almost every single person that I am going to talk about in this book is dead. They have 'shuffled off this mortal coil' as Hamlet would put it, although I've always thought that was a bit of an over the top way of saying it. Then again, Hamlet isn't really the character one goes to for a rational, low-key quote.

Anyway, there is no doubt that Pras was dead. This must be distinctly understood, or nothing wonderful can come of the story I am going to relate. No, hold on, that's Marley. Pras is very simply, unliteraturely[6], dead.

Upon his death, the Romans conveniently forgot about any agreement they had made about sharing the kingdom with Pras' daughters, and they didn't stop there. I will hand things over to the great Roman historian Tacitus, who I think gives a perfect description of what happened next:

> *"His dominions were ravaged by the centurions; the slaves pillaged his house, and his effects were seized as lawful plunder. His wife, Boudicca, was disgraced with cruel stripes; her daughters were*

---

[5] Or possibly 60 AD – the date isn't clear, but nearly 2000 years have passed since then, a few months isn't going to make much different to this story!

[6] I know it isn't a word. But it should be!

12

ravished, and the most illustrious of the Icenians were, by force, deprived of the positions which had been transmitted to them by their ancestors. The whole country was considered as a legacy bequeathed to the plunderers. The relations of the deceased king were reduced to slavery."

There you have it. The best contemporary historical source we have for what happened to Boudicca. 'Disgraced with cruel stripes' is Tacitus' slightly poetic way of telling us that she was whipped. Many versions of the story have the daughters raped in front of Boudicca, although this isn't clear from Tacitus' account of things. Even so, before you feel too sorry for Boudicca (and you should feel a bit sorry for her), wait until you hear what her army does to people a little later on!

Interestingly, in his account of the uprising Cassius Dio - another Roman historian, but one who was writing over a hundred years after the event - doesn't mention this rape or whipping at all, instead for him the uprising is caused because of money. Is this, perhaps, because he didn't want to include such violence in his histories? The answer there is no, he has plenty of descriptions of violence coming up! Perhaps it was because he was writing in a very pro-Roman style, whereas Tacitus is actually very good at writing his history, if not without bias, then at least with a nod to the point of view of the peoples the Romans invaded. Or possibly Cassius discovered it never happened, although as this would destroy a major aspect of this legend - reducing it to a fight over money - I think we should let that possibility lie for the moment.

So now finally we get to the really exciting piece of the story – Boudicca's comeback. She has been whipped, and had her land plundered, her daughters have been raped in front of her. The Roman army is huge and she has no real chance of defeating them, this is the point where she ought by rights to be a completely broken woman.

She isn't, however. Like the heroine in a Hollywood blockbuster, just as all seems lost she picks herself back up. Although history does not record a training montage at this point in time, I think is clear from the context that she must have gone through a montage, with a heavy 80s rock soundtrack playing as Boudicca gathered the Trinovantes tribe from Essex[7] and began a march towards Camulodunum (modern day Colchester), while the main Roman force and the Governor Suetonius were in North Wales hunting down rebels.

Camulodunum was destroyed by the army of Boudicca, and the temple there managed to hold on for only two days before that too fell to the army of rebels. They then marched on to Londonium (London, at that time a small, new settlement) and carried out the same methodical destruction.

The treatment of the defeated enemy by Boudicca, according to Tacitus and Dio, is not going to inspire a lot or support for her cause at this point. Tacitus has them putting people to *'halter and gibbet, slaughter and defoliation, fire and sword'*. Dio, however, provides a much more Tarantino style description of the way that Boudicca's army treated defeated enemies, and especially the women. If you are reading this book while enjoying anything to eat, have a faint heart, or are under the age of eighteen, I would suggest you skip the next paragraph:

> *"The worst and most bestial atrocity committed by their captors was the following. They hung up naked the noblest and most distinguished women and then cut off their breasts and sewed them to their mouths, in order to make the victims appear to be eating them; afterwards they impaled the women on sharp skewers run lengthwise through the entire body."*

See. That is just sick. If you feel ill now, then I'm sorry, but I did warn you in advance. Hopefully most of you will have become too desensitised to violence by films and violent video games to actually be vomiting at this point in time, because I don't think the publishing budget for this book is going to extend to dry wipe pages.

Of course, whether or not this actually happened is another key question. It is likely that Boudicca's army would have killed

---

[7] Who presumably wore fake tan where the other tribes wore the blue woad war paint.

everybody in the places they defeated, they were not in a situation where taking prisoners and holding them was an option. However the particular details of the savagery here are likely to be just as much the result of rumour, legend, and a general view of the Britons as uncivilised barbarians.

The rebel army marched on and struck Verulamium (St Albans) next, but by this point in time Suetonius was almost back from Wales with his army, and was gathering as many troops as he could to crush the uprising.

The two armies met near Atherstone in Warwickshire... or near Messing in Essex… or in Leicestershire. or Northamptonshire. Basically the two armies met in a location that today is unknown, and lost in a web of legend with various places laying claim to the final battle, and archaeological evidence providing no definitive proof.

Unfortunately when dealing with an uprising in Roman Britain, even one as legendary as this, the actual facts are rather thin on the ground, relying as we do on Tacitus as the closest thing to a contemporary source we have, and his account was written about fifty years after the events.

From here we know that the battle was fairly one sided – according to Tacitus (for what it is worth) only four hundred Romans died compared with eighty thousand Britons. Although these figures are likely to be far from accurate, we can be pretty sure that it was an overwhelming victory. The skill, discipline and tactics of the Roman Army are themselves legendary, and against an army of wild Britons from various tribes with no formal training, they were devastating.

Boudicca, according to accounts, and to legend, refused to be captured and mistreated by the Romans again, and instead decided to drink poison and kill herself. Thus ended the uprising led by Boudicca, on an now unknown battlefield, and she was buried in an unknown location – although urban folklore has it that she lies buried under platform 10 at King's Cross Station, just ¼ of a platform from the Hogwarts Express.

So there we have it, Queen Boudicca of the Iceni – a genuine Warrior Queen, wrapped up in legend, folklore and mysteries. Not the only strong woman in history – or even in this book – but certainly one of the most powerful female warrior leaders in English history!

Seahenge
(To Stay or To Go)

I'm sitting down to begin work on this chapter on a late November day on the Isle of Wight. I say 'day', but at just before half past four it is already dark outside, so perhaps it is already night. My dog, Shazu, is curled up in the chair where she has sat most of the day - occasionally opening her eyes to look at the grey, rainy day outside the window which has kept me in with the computer and books, rather than down running on the beach with her. In fact it has been a week of weather like this. What walks we have gone out on have been muddy, damp, and spent surveying the damage and broken branches caused by the winds - and we have more severe weather warnings coming in for tonight.

As soon as we get a relatively clear day we will walk the mile or so to the beach and see how bad the cliff falls have been; how much further back and in how many places the cliffs of the back of the Wight have been eroded away. I go walking along the beach quite often, and always keep my eyes open in case one day I spot a dinosaur bone (possible, considering the number found on the island, but unlikely considering my lack of knowledge as far as palaeontology is concerned), some old artefact long buried in the cliffs (again possible, but the odds of anything coming to the surface that isn't immediately washed out to sea are sparse), or a standing circle similar to Stonehenge (practically impossible!).

The mention of a standing circle next to the mentions of small artefacts may seem like a silly piece of hyperbole - an exaggeration in the extreme as to what sort of thing might suddenly reveal itself owing to a spell of bad weather altering the island and the line between land and sea. In a way it is.

However, far off in the distant land of Norfolk, somewhere near King's Lynn[8], erosion and a changing landscape in 1998 revealed a ritual circle, not of standing stones, but of wooden posts, within the eroding dunes on the beach.

In 2049BC, a little over 4060 years ago, oak trees were felled, worked and positioned to make a circle of 55 posts, with a large stump in the centre, for the purposes of... well... something. Probably something religious - it is not clear what. Probably not a central location, because even though they weren't at sea when built the location would still have been a salt marsh. For this reason some people have suggested that it may have been a place to leave corpses for excarnation (the flesh being removed) before burial elsewhere, although there is currently no more evidence for this that for any other purpose.

Much like Stonehenge (from which this circle of wood has derived its name, despite not being a henge at all - for people who care, a 'Henge' must have an earth bank with a ditch inside) we may never be certain of the use of Seahenge. Also like Stonehenge, some modern day Druids have claimed a deep significance to the site, despite the fact that in truth they have no more idea of the sites meaning or purpose than anybody else. They do, however, have a right to their religion if it does not affect other people or the safety of this important monument. In the same way that archaeologists examining a site must limit damage and preserve an ancient site, monument or artefact as much as possible.

Herein lays the problem with Seahenge. Because of the particular way that it was covered and preserved owing to a change in the area from salt marsh to a freshwater wetland area, it was covered in peat, and finally with sand. The peat (as with 'peat bog men') preserved the wood by protecting it from oxygen and therefore most of the rot causing microorganisms. As circumstances had changed again, and the water had eroded the peat until Seahenge was visible and exposed to the air, which led to its 'discovery', it was now in danger of rotting and being destroyed

---

[8] Or even nearer to Holme-Next-The Sea, but I didn't know where that was. To be honest I couldn't immediately place King's Lynn on a map (although I did know Norfolk!), but I thought you were more likely to know the city!

and eventually washed away - leading to a very difficult decision and a great deal of controversy.

In essence the decision was simple. Either to leave Seahenge in situ, where it could stand as it had for over 4000 years, until it rotted and was lost permanently, or move it away from its position to allow the wood to be treated and preserved. If it was left in situ people would be able to see it as it was, perhaps it could be helped it survive a little longer, but nobody would be tampering and moving Seahenge. Druid protesters saw moving the timbers of Seahenge as sacrilegious, as they claimed that this must have been a religious site at some point and so should be left alone - although again I point out, without wishing to cause offence, that they did not know the site existed, nor what the monument was built for, and even if it was a religious site it was not 'their' religious site. If they were protecting it just because they believe you should not move any religious site I hope that there are druids protesting any church that closes. That however is slightly to one side of the point, and a can of worms to be opened on another day.

There were of course lots of groups of people who wanted the posts to stay on site, including businesses, local people who enjoyed seeing it there, and, I have no doubt, the English Heritage themselves, who finally made the difficult decision to remove it for preservation. I can see why all of these people would have wanted it untouched.

A couple of miles from my house on the island there are a pair of Neolithic monumental stones, one standing and one fallen, known as Mottistone Longstone. They are, these days, just objects in the landscape. In the past they have been used as a centre for tribal meetings, and probably also for religious reasons. There is a barrow leading off from them which they are probably related to in some way, possibly forming an entrance.

If someone suggested these stones were going to be taken away I would not be happy about it. As far as possible ancient monuments should be left where they are because something would be lost if they moved these stones to a museum – you would lose all the impact of their position on the downs. They would just become two large rocks.

However, this is not a great comparison, because they are unlikely to be threatened at the moment. In a few hundred, or a few thousand years they may well be – they are probably only a mile or so from the coast where I will go walking to see how bad the cliff falls and erosion have been, which means that there will come a day when these ancient monuments stand at the edge of the cliff, and the decision will have to be made whether to leave them to fall into the sea, or to move them. At that point in time I think they would be better off preserved in a museum, in a replica landscape, than lost to the ocean. There will be people then who say they should be left alone and it will be difficult. Nobody will want them to go, but some people will think it is a necessary evil to preserve the stones in some form.

I am certain, from the place I have visited, and the people I have met at English Heritage sites, that had leaving the wooden monument in situ and preserving it been an option at all, that they would have done it. As it happens, to leave it there would have meant the loss of Seahenge altogether, and that would, I think, have been far worse than the loss of moving it out of position. The move was handled carefully, photographs and exact details taken. Every piece of wood from Seahenge was taken, examined, and spent nearly a decade at the Mary Rose Trust to allow the wood to be treated in a similar manner to the timbers of the Mary Rose itself.

Now Seahenge is on display once more in a museum in King's Lynn. It is close to home, but it is not home. It will, however, live on, thanks to the preservation work.

Not far from the site of Seahenge a second circle was found, and named Holme II. This was left where it was, possibly as a result of the backlash and protests about the removal of the first one. If you wish to see any of it then be very quick, the last report I have seen on it shows very little left visible, and uses the words 'The, now lost, Bronze Age timbers'.

There will always be controversy. We cannot save every single piece of archaeology, every building or monument. We shouldn't move monuments if it can be avoided and they are in no danger. Personally, however, I'm glad that I will still be able to go and see Seahenge in some form when I have a show up near King's Lynn sometime. I will not be able to see Henge II.

That is why, if I go for walk along the beach in a few days and find something fantastic or interesting, I will do my best to make sure every detail of its location is recorded, and that it is then removed to a museum before it is lost to the sea.

Princes in the Tower
Richard III on trial

Back in about 1997, when I was in year eight at the Billericay School in Essex, I remember a teacher coming up to me after a history lesson, and mentioning to me an extra-curricular activity that was available. The chance to prepare a case, to be played out in a lesson, in which we would put Richard III on trial for the murder of Edward V and his younger brother Richard in 1483. This happened to coincide with me going into hospital[9], and I had hours free in the hospital room waiting for the operation, during which I could study the pile of documents I had been given to prepare my case. To my surprise, looking back now, I can't remember whether I was the prosecution or the defence in the case, what I do remember very clearly is that I was declared the winner, having managed to prove my case to a level acceptable in a court of law - or at least to the students who made up the jury.

Now I come to think of like that, I think I was probably the defence. I seem to remember pointing out that he could only be found guilty if it was 'beyond all reasonable doubt', and I don't think there is any case I could have made that was that watertight. In a court of law I think Richard III would certainly not have been condemned for the crime. He isn't, however, facing a court of law in this book. He faces the judgement of history, and history and people reading it can pass judgement based on the fact that something looks likely, rather than having to prove it beyond reasonable doubt.

I think the fairest way for me to approach the subject then, is to go back in my own life, to that fictitious court in the classroom. I will provide you with a prosecution lawyer and a defence lawyer. I

---

[9] Don't worry, dear readers. It was only an ingrowing toenail – I'm fine now!

will provide a judge, and as far as possible I will provide witnesses to speak for themselves. I will provide evidence, and I will provide a case like in all the best courtroom dramas. What I will not provide is a jury. I will leave that to you. You can decide what level of proof you need to declare guilt, or to find him innocent. So now let me declare this court in session, the honourable Judge Greg presiding[10].

Judge Greg: We are gathered here today to…

Council for The Defence: Excuse me your honour. This is a trial, not a wedding.

Judge Greg: I know that, but I don't know the correct way to start a trail and can't be bothered to research it. Now stop pointing out inaccuracies in the book or I'll hold you in contempt of court.

Defence: Yes, your honour.

Judge Greg: Good. We are gathered here today to try Richard III, King from 6th July 1483 to August 22nd 1485, for the crime or murder on two counts. The murder of two children, his nephews, held in the Tower Of London; Edward V and Edward's younger brother Richard, Duke of York. Perhaps the Council for the Prosecution can start us off.

Prosecution: Thank you your honour. And may I just say how incredibly handsome your honour is looking today.

Judge Greg: Of course you may. But don't waste any more time telling me what I already know. What is your case?

Prosecution: Your honour, the prosecution…

Defence: Objection, your honour.

Judge Greg: What?

Defence: Your honour, I just wanted to note that the constant use of the words 'Your honour', although setting this clearly as

---

[10] What? You thought I was going to cast myself in anything but the top job?

a courtroom scene and artificially increasing the word count for the book, is also beginning to get a little tedious.

Judge Greg: Objection sustained, this court no longer wishes to hear the words 'Your honour'.

Prosecution: As your lordship pleases.

Judge Greg: Don't push it. Get on with the case.

Prosecution: I will prove that King Richard III of England arranged for his two Nephews, Edward IV and Richard, Duke of York, to be murdered in the Tower Of London. I will make the case that they were smothered under the orders of the King, and were then buried at the bottom of some stairs in the Tower. He did this in order to…

Judge Greg: Yes, yes, we'll get to that. Defence?

Defence: I, on the other hand, will prove that any suggestion that Richard III killed the Princes in the Tower is based on poor evidence and speculation. The 'fact' that the Princes were murdered at all is in itself questionable, and that, even if they were murdered, Richard's motive for such a crime would be far less than others. We will maintain that the accusation itself is nothing more than a smear campaign aimed at Richard by Henry Tudor, Sir Thomas More, and one William Shakespeare.

Judge Greg: The playwright?

Defence: No, the inventor of the level-winding fishing reel. Of course the playwright!

Judge Greg: One more smart alec comment from you and I'll declare the defendant guilty.

Defence: Well that is exactly the point I was aiming to make! The Defendant has been declared guilty of the crime by people in power without evidence, just because they had their own personal reasons for vilifying King Richard.

Judge Greg: Hold on, just to clarify, this is Richard the Lionheart, right?

Prosecution: No. That was Richard I. This is Richard III, the one with the hunch, limp and withered arm who murdered his nephews in the Town of London.

Defence: Objection! He didn't murder them. And the hunch, limp and withered arm are all false descriptions made by Richard's enemies and made famous by Shakespeare. Who was, let's point out, a writer of plays and fictions for entertainment – not a historian!

Judge Greg: Well I hardly think this book can have a go at anyone for writing about history flexibly for entertainment purposes! However I think it would be very politically incorrect of us to judge the King based on his physical appearance, so I will rule that irrelevant to the case.

Prosecution: Very well. Shall I call my first witness?

Judge Greg: Please do!

Prosecution: I call to the stand Sir Thomas More, Lawyer, Author and Statesman 1478-1535, and writer of 'History of King Richard III'.

Sir Thomas: Good Morning.

Prosecution: In your book, 'History of Richard III' you make the first recorded accusation that Richard III killed the Princes?

Sir Thomas: That is correct.

Prosecution: For what reason would the King have killed the Princes?

Sir Thomas: Originally Edward V had been declared King, on the death of his father. There was a highly questionable suggestion that the Princes may have been illegitimate, which ruled them out of the line of succession, and so Richard was declared King instead. However the young Princes still held a claim if the accusation of illegitimacy could be proved false, and would also have been a rallying point for any rebellion. In that period the crown was hotly contested, and so he had a strong political motivation to remove the Princes permanently.

Prosecution: And what evidence do you have?

Sir Thomas: One of the men that carried out the murder confessed in 1502.

Prosecution: And this was Sir James Tyrell?

Sir Thomas: That is correct. He confessed that he, John Dighton and Miles Forest, working on orders from King Richard smothered the Prices with pillows.

Prosecution: And what happened to the bodies?

Sir Thomas: They were buried at the foot of a stairway in the tower.

Prosecution: The foot of a stairway where two children's bodies were subsequently found in 1674?

Sir Thomas: I can't comment on events after my death.

Prosecution: But you accept that it is likely that if bodies were found at the foot of the stairs, of children the correct age, buried in the correct period, that these would be the bodies you report having been buried there?

Defence: Objection!

Judge Greg: Prosecution, you can't question the witness about events after his death. We must have some rules!

Prosecution: I withdraw the question. No further questions your honour.

Judge Greg: Defence, do you have any questions?

Defence: Yes. Good morning Sir Thomas. I'd like to address some of the points raised by my colleague in a moment. Before that though, I'd just like to establish a bit of background about you?

Prosecution: Objection! The witness isn't on trial!

Defence: I am going to attempt to prove the possibility that this witness is biased, an important consideration in a court of history!

Judge Greg: That sounds fair. Proceed.

Defence: Sir Thomas, I believe you were born in 1478.

Prosecution: Objection – the witness's date of birth has already been established.

Judge Greg: Is this going somewhere?

Defence: I only wish to point out that this makes Sir Thomas only 5 at the time of the alleged murders, and therefore he has no first hand involvement or knowledge of the events.

Judge Greg: Your point has been made. Proceed with a different question.

Defence: Who was King when you wrote your history?

Sir Thomas: Henry VIII.

Defence: For whom you were a close advisor I believe?

Sir Thomas: That is correct.

Defence: And that is Henry VIII, son of Henry VII, the man who became King after defeating Richard III at the Battle of Bosworth?

Sir Thomas: That is correct.

Defence: And so you would concede that there was a political motive for besmirching the name of Richard III, and at the same time claiming that the young Prices, who could have had a better claim to the throne than Henry, were both dead.

Prosecution: Objection!

Judge Greg: Sustained. Your suggestion of bias is taken into account Defence, but we cannot make Sir Thomas confess to it in this book as we have no evidence that he ever did!

Defence: Very well. Sir Thomas, you say that Sir James Tyrell confessed to the murders?

Sir Thomas: That is correct.

Defence: So he was executed for treason and murdering royalty?

Sir Thomas: No.

Defence: No? He supposedly confessed to murdering two Princes and he was not punished for the crime in the appropriate manner for that time?

Sir Thomas: No... but I can't give you the reason why not – that decision wouldn't have been anything to do with me. I was just recording the history.

Defence: And it doesn't seem strange to you?

Prosecution: Objection!

Defence: I withdraw the question. Now of course the case of the prosecution is weakened by the fact that there is a lack of evidence that the Princes were murdered at all, aside from the fact that it is recorded that they were no longer seen after mid-June 1483. The prosecution will make much of the fact that two children's bodies were found at the bottom of a staircase in the Tower in the 1674, which he has already brought to your attention.

Sir Thomas: He has, yes.

Defence: You wrote in your history that the bodies were buried, and I quote, "at the stayre foote, metely depe in the grounde under a heap of stones". That is correct?

Sir Thomas: It is.

Defence: The prosecution tries to use this as evidence that these bodies are the bodies of the Princes. However, I note that later on in your book you state that the bodies were removed and reburied in an unknown location.

Sir Thomas: That is correct.

Defence: So according to your book the bodies at the bottom of the tower could not have been the Princes?

Sir Thomas: I do not know where they were buried after that.

Defence: But it is unlikely that they would have been buried under another staircase?

Sir Thomas: I cannot say. The priest who reburied them died without saying where they were buried.

Defence: Thereby inconveniently making the one piece of evidence which would have confirmed the Princes were dead unavailable to you and all of Henry's accusers.

Prosecution: Objection. That isn't a question.

Judge Greg: Sustained.

Defence: No further questions.

Judge Greg: Sir Thomas, you are free to go.

I would just like to clear up the matter of these bones before we proceed if I may. These bones were found in 1674. Were they examined since then?

Prosecution: Yes. In 1933 the bones were forensically examined and found to be the bones of two children of the right age.

Judge Greg: Two boys?

Defence: No. The gender of the bones wasn't able to be established at that time. The bones have not been subsequently tested, and no DNA tests have been done on the bones.

Judge Greg: But two boys went missing, and two skeletons have been found in a location that is appropriate?

Defence: We will acknowledge that skeletons have been found, but there is no real evidence to suggest that these are the bones of the Princes.

Judge Greg: Very well, we will leave that evidence for the jury to decide. Prosecution, any more witnesses?

Prosecution: The prosecution rests on this evidence. We believe that we have shown a confession by the murderer working on behalf of King Richard; we have found bones which the defence accepts could be the bones of the Princes. We have also proved a strong motive for the murders. This is the evidence on which history has generally found Richard guilty for over five hundred years. Also Shakespeare said he was guilty, and Shakespeare is obviously great.

Judge: An eloquent summary. Defence, you have a couple of witnesses – not too many mind; remember this is a condensed trial in a condensed history.

Defence: Very well. For my first witness I call Robert Stillington, Bishop of Bath and Wells from 1465 to 1491, a courtier to Edward IV, and one of the men who helped in putting Richard III on the throne. Good afternoon.

Bishop: Good afternoon.

Judge Greg: Has this chapter been going on that long?

Defence: Bishop, you are partly responsible for getting Richard III to the throne of England?

Bishop: I am, yes.

Defence: Did he come to power as the result of the disappearance of the Princes from the Tower?

Bishop: No. His claim to the throne was made at a period when the children were still seen playing in the grounds by a number of people. His was a legal claim.

Defence: Based on?

Bishop: As brother of the old King, Edward IV, he was the first in line, once it was ruled that the two Princes were illegitimate.

Defence: In what way illegitimate? Were they not Edward IV's children?

Bishop: I would not dare to suggest such a thing. We are confident the children were born to King Edward IV by the woman known as Queen Elizabeth Woodville. However it came to light that in 1461, 3 years prior to the wedding between Edward and Elizabeth, that King Edward IV had secretly married Lady Elizabeth Talbot. She was still alive at the time of the wedding between Edward and Elizabeth, and therefore that marriage was illegal.

Defence: Making the two boys bastards and...

Prosecution: Objection! He can't call the boys names!

Defence: I was using the word 'bastard' in its correct historical usage to mean a child born out of wedlock.

Judge Greg: But also because you thought it would be funny to swear in a courtroom?

Defence: I guess.

Judge Greg: Well don't say 'bastard' again.

Defence: Yes, Judge. Making the two Princes illegitimate, and therefore removing any claim to the throne?

Bishop: That is correct.

Defence: No further questions.

Judge Greg: Prosecution, any cross examination?

Prosecution: I'll ask some questions, but I won't be cross!

Judge Greg: For that appalling joke I find you in contempt of court and sentence you to a night in the cells.

Prosecution: That sounds fair. Bishop, did people dispute the suggestion that the Princes were illegitimate?

Bishop: The ruling was made in law that...

Prosecution: Please listen to the question. Did anybody dispute the claim?

Bishop: Yes, the enemies of Richard tried to pretend that...

Prosecution: So simply declaring the Princes illegitimate did not rule out any attempt to get them back on the throne?

Bishop: Well, no, but...

Prosecution: No further questions.

Judge Greg: Well played that man. A wonderful piece of courtroom drama! Any further witnesses defence?

Defence: I shall call one more surprise witness! I call to the stand Richard Plantagenet!

Judge Greg: Who?

Defence: A man who, I will claim, is none other than Richard, Duke of York, the younger of the two Princes, grown to manhood and therefore not dead in a tower!

Judge Greg: Oh gosh, that is exciting!

Prosecution: That's cheating. You can't call one of the murdered Princes to give evidence that he wasn't murdered! There is no proof that they grew up!

Defence: I will aim to show reasonable proof that at least one of them did, and therefore reasonable doubt that a murder even took place! Good afternoon Mr Plantagenet.

Mr Plantagenet: 'Allo there!

Defence: Can I ask your occupation and where you worked circa 1538?

Mr Plantagenet: I was a bricklayer at St John's Abbey in Colchester.

Defence: And you happen to share a name with the young Duke of York supposedly murdered?

Mr Plantagenet: I do.

Defence: And you speak Latin – uncommon in a bricklayer isn't that?

Mr Plantagenet: It certainly is. I'm the only one I know that does.

Defence: More fitting to a man who has a claim to the throne - someone that was placed into some form of medieval witness protection programme?

Prosecution: Objection! This is all speculation!

Defence: So is the prosecution case!

Prosecution: Is not!

Defence: Is too!

Prosecution: Is…

Judge Greg: Enough! I'm calling an end to this farce of a court case - and to this chapter as soon as I have offered my summary for the jury.

My dear reader, you have heard some of the evidence involved in this case, enough I would hope for you at the very least not to dismiss the possibility of Richard's innocence out of hand. To what extent we need complete proof of guilt in history is up to your conscience to decide, as it is up to you to decide whether it actually matters this far down the line.

The main points I would most like you to take away from this chapter is that everybody who writes a book or gives evidence in any historical dispute like this, including, I suppose, myself, is, either deliberately or accidently, going to be adding their personal opinions into the evidence. Therefore if the 'truth' of any historical or modern debate, or court case, should be important to you, you must listen to both sides of the argument fully and carefully, and not just one source or newspaper.

That is my summary as Judge. Now I'm going to go and get drunk as a Lord. All rise, the court is now closed.

Howard Carter
The Man Who Found a Pharaoh

Usually when we look at a monument, an artefact, a burial chamber or even a lost city that has been discovered, it is so amazing and interesting that the man who discovered it is largely lost to history. Do you know the name of the man who found the Mary Rose? How about the name of the man who discovered Pompeii?[11]

There is, however, one discovery where the man who discovered it is nearly as famous (in England at least), as his greatest discovery, and whose story is nearly as interesting. The man is Howard Carter, and he found the tomb of the Pharaoh Tutankhamen, and as a result he is one of the most famous archaeologists of all time. In fact, a quick survey of famous archaeologists puts the top three as Indiana Jones (despite being fictional), Howard Carter, and 'Mick' from 'Time Team', narrowly beating Phil by virtue of his jumpers[12].

If I'm honest I did worry that I might be cheating slightly on this chapter, stretching the subtitle of 'Histories from England' almost to breaking point, by taking us into the deserts of Egypt among the mummies and Pharaohs. I wondered if perhaps I should really leave the topic for another book entirely.

Howard Carter was, however, an Englishman, which makes him fit in. Also I can't be certain, however much I hope, that this book will do well enough to justify a second volume[13]. If it doesn't

---

[11] If you do then get in touch – we need to form a pub quiz team! Just need a sports guy!

[12] The survey was of 2 people, one being me and the other my dog, who actually prefers Phil. For the record it was conducted while watching back to back Time Team episodes in the background on More4 while I type, as a break from the back to back Top Gear and QI over on Dave.

do well enough, and I'd left out Howard Carter, I would really feel that I had left you without an important person from English history and a figure that played an important role in my life as a historian – if historian is the right word for what I'm doing here.

I want to take you back, if I can, to about 1994. The world is a different place back then. We had two computers in our primary school, and they took floppy disks - and not those silly little so called floppy disks, but the slightly older 5 ¼" disks that preceded even them. It's probably in a museum now. There was no internet, mobile phones were the size of bricks and owned only by a select few, and the teachers still wrote on blackboards (and were allowed to call them that).

In this far off past there was a young boy, in year five, standing 120.5 cm tall[14]. He was clever, cheeky, and apt to be lazy a lot of the time – a nice, smart boy who 'could try harder', to paraphrase almost every school report I ever got. I often get the impression that this could be a summary report of my life as well, except maybe without the 'nice' sometimes.

This boy, being in year 5, had already studied the Tudors and Stewarts, and had nurtured a fascination with dinosaurs for many years. If you had asked him he probably would have said he wanted to be a palaeontologist –a long word he would have known since the release of Jurassic Park in 1993. However this year he was destined to move away from dinosaurs, and 'Alan Grant', and move to an interest in human history and archaeology, with Howard Carter and Indiana Jones as his new key heroes in that field.

---

[13] Thank you for buying this book – you've helped me push towards the point where it will be worth me trying to publish another one. Unless you stole this book, borrowed a friend's, or downloaded an illegal copy off the internet, in which case I hope you'll make it up to me by buying a copy of the next book… and a ticket to one of my shows… and any merchandise I release. Or just your own copy of this book. Whatever!

[14] I say tall, but in fact the height leaps so readily to mind because I was incredibly proud of being the shortest boy in my year.

So what, to a 9 year old boy, could replace the CG dinosaurs (at that time cutting edge) and tales of these gigantic creatures that had held his fascination since seeing the massive diplodocus skeleton in the Natural History Museum some years before[15]. There are really two answers – one is the pyramids - but above and beyond that is mummies!

Beyond all of the treasures and jewels found within the tomb of Tutankhamen, it is still the idea of the preservation of the mummy, along with the area around him, that still fascinates me, and it was Howard Carter's description of first opening the tomb - which I have read countless times since - that really gave me the idea that in archaeology you could discover so much more than just the dry bones you could with dinosaurs; under the right circumstances you can step, even if only for a second, into the past.

"At first I could see nothing, the hot air escaping from the chamber causing the candle flames to flicker, but presently, as my eyes grew accustomed to the light, details of the room within emerged slowly from the mist, strange animals, statues and gold - everywhere the glint of gold.

For the moment - an eternity it must have seemed to the others standing by - I was dumb with amazement, and when Lord Carnarvon, unable to stand the suspense any longer, inquired anxiously, 'Can you see anything?' it was all I could do to get out the words, 'Yes, wonderful things.'"

The gory details of the making of mummies, of Egyptian Gods, and the life of the young Pharaoh Tutankhamen really are well beyond the remit of this book, and I hope I will get another chance to revisit them in the future in a book on Egypt. For now I think that the story of how this young Englishman finally found himself looking in and seeing these 'wonderful things', in a tomb he had spent much of his adult life searching for, makes an interesting enough story in its own right.

Originally Carter had been trained by his father to follow in his footsteps and become an artist, and so this is where Carter's career began, before making the gradual slide over into becoming an

---

[15] I still feel betrayed since the day that I discovered that that is in fact a replica skeleton.

archaeologist - a feeling I know only too well. When I left school I was going to be a 'serious actor' doing Shakespeare and stuff, before my own slide into comic acting, then a bit of magic, comedy performing, writing and escapology. Something I'll touch on a little more in a later chapter.

The slide could arguably be said to have begun when the young Howard Carter accompanied his father (who was painting a portrait) to the home of Lord Amherst, who owned a vast collection of Ancient Egyptian artefacts, which he allowed Howard to look at. Howard grew closer to the Amherst family, even after his father's portrait of Lord Amherst was complete.

Howard spent a lot of time sketching the artefacts, which led, in 1891 when Howard was 17, to him being offered a job sketching the artwork within tombs for the Egypt Exploration Fund. He first carried out a short training period at the British Museum, and then went out to Egypt itself. So it was as an artist and not an excavator that Howard Carter first arrived in Egypt, and he worked hard at the somewhat tedious task of copying all of the tomb decorations onto parchment, so that they could then be taken away and studied in England or elsewhere.

His hard work led to him being sent early in 1892 to train as an excavator, and he rapidly developed his skills as an archaeologist to become the overseer of a whole site and from there, by the time he was 25, he was given the job of Inspector General of Monuments for Upper Egypt, giving him the job of watching over and regulating all of the excavations which were taking place at that time in the Nile Valley.

This was a very prominent job, and one which could have seen the peak of his career was it not for the very old English habit of going to war with the French, albeit on a small scale. In 1905 a bunch of drunken French tourists started creating trouble in the camp where they were all based, and Carter gave his guards in the camp permission to use force to defend themselves. This led to complaints to higher authorities, and (with Carter's stubborn refusal to apologise) Carter being removed to an out of the way dig site, and his resignation from the job.

Carter went back to art, not having any family money with which to sustain himself, let alone fund a dig. He had heard by this point about a Pharaoh named King Tut, to whom only one reference had been found, owing to the fact that Tutankhamen's successors in the role of Pharaoh attempted to have him retrospectively expunged from history by chiselling his name off all monuments, and burying him in a small tomb instead of the originally designated tomb he had designed for himself. Carter strongly believed that this Pharaoh was still buried somewhere in the Valley Of The Kings, the vast area riddled with 'hidden' tombs, where Pharaohs had been buried in since it became clear that the pyramids were too much of an advertisement to tomb robbers.

It was in 1908 that Carter met Lord Carnarvon, the man who would be there to ask "Can you see anything?" when the tomb of Tutankhamen was opened, and who would fund Carter's digs, losing money over the years until the eventual success.

Lord Carnarvon's faith in Carter's ability to find the tomb, as well as Carter's faith in himself, is very important to the fact that they kept searching for the tomb. This was at a point when most people believed that every tomb in the Valley of the Kings had been discovered, and Carnarvon had been funding Carter's digs for over a decade. In fact, by 1922 Lord Carnarvon had had enough and told Carter that he would not be funding another dig.

Carter, with all the skill of a carnival games hustler, managed to convince Lord Carnarvon to have just one more go – funding one final dig, to which Lord Carnarvon, fortunately, agreed. Carter's final chance to find King Tut's tomb began with the new dig season on November 1st 1922. Almost immediately (within three days) a step was found – a step which would prove eventually to lead down to the tomb of Tutankhamen.

From there the dig went well, despite a few predictable delays, including at one stage Carter re-covering the staircase as he waited for Lord Carnarvon to arrive from England to witness the opening of the tomb. Eventually, however they stood there and broke open the door at the bottom of the staircase to reveal a room full of rubble. Someone had been there before them - this was clear from tamper marks on some of the seals - and it was another long wait as the rubble was removed by Carter's team of workers, to reveal a second door.

Carter has been attacked on occasion over the years, and accused of stealing items from the tomb (he didn't) and of not treating the tomb with respect. The fact that once the rubble was clear he took the time, as he had learnt long ago, to carefully draw and photograph the second door that they uncovered, and carefully detailed everything in the tomb at all points[16].

The second door was the one, which when opened, contained Howard Carter's 'Wonderful things', which included the throne of King Tut, and gold and valuable objects galore. Once again everything was photographed and recorded to avoid theft, and then another, hidden door was opened. And in the next room, finally, Howard Carter found the burial place of King Tutankhamen!

This being a condensed history I have somewhat rushed through the story of Carter's search, and yet I hope that already I have managed to convey something of the length of time that he spent looking for something that almost everybody else told him wasn't there. The contents of the tomb, as I say, are really for another book, and if you can't wait for me to write one I strongly

---

[16] He did, unfortunately, damage the mummy when it was found. He did so in order to remove the mummy from where resin had solidly locked it into the coffin, and he had attempted other ways of removing it first. These days there would have been no question of removing the mummy in this way, but back then technology was limited. Today we could have scanned the mummy and found ways, if deemed necessary, to remove the resin with care. The same as the way that in 2005 the mummy was given a CT scan causing no damage, whereas in 1925 when the mummy was given an autopsy and unwrapped by a Professor and Doctor trained and practiced in such procedures, it resulted in the mummy's head being detached, along with other limbs and a piece of ear. The main damage to the body, therefore, was not done by Carter, but by the autopsy, which was performed in front of not just Carter, but also people from the Antiquities Department and officials from the Egyptian Government, none of whom saw fit to halt the autopsy at any point.

recommend you go out and find another now while you wait – there are hundreds of books written about Carter and Tutankhamen. If you do you'll even be able to have a smug sense of superiority when I get around to writing a condensed history of Egypt, and you know so much more about it than I will have room to fit in there!

In the meantime just remember that sometimes the story of the discoverer can be as exciting as the discovery, and that sometimes you have to hold on to your beliefs if you are going to achieve anything. However, if you are in a casino or playing a game at a carnival, know when to quit!

Origins of the English Civil War

Why the Cavaliers fought the Roundheads

I'm hoping that having got this far into this book, which has specified that it is about English history, that none of you will have got a bit huffy about my reference to the 'English Civil War', as opposed to the 'British Civil War' or (as I hear it is being called by some historians these days) the 'War Of The Three Nations'. Presumably these are the same historians who use the terms 'CE' (Common Era) and 'BCE' (Before Common Era) instead of 'BC' and 'AD' because the original terms are too 'religious' ('Before Christ' and 'Anno Domini) and either may offend someone, or is a dating system based on an unproven figure.

However I think this is pointless – changing the terms we use doesn't change the basis of the dating system. In fact I'll go further and say that it is wrong – it is a deliberate attempt by certain 'historians' to hide the history of the Gregorian Calendar which we use. That is why I still use BC and AD despite the fact that Jesus (if such a historical figure existed) almost certainly wasn't born in the year 1AD. (Part of my reasons for writing that is to annoy my brother, who got very annoyed when I pointed out that Herod, who is supposed to have killed all of the baby boys in the area of Bethlehem after the birth of Jesus - according to the Bible only, no other sources suggest he committed this particular massacre - actually died in the year 4BC).

The English Civil War, however, is not the same as the 'British Civil War', but is in fact a part of the larger whole, with slightly different results and battles, although the line of what can be defined as the 'English' and 'British' Civil War is fairly loose, and

41

there is a lot of crossover, and I am going to quite blatantly cross backwards and forwards over that line throughout this chapter.

All of this preamble, therefore, is basically my way of slightly mitigating the fact that in order to fit this 'war' into my English Histories I have used the title that suits my purposes best, despite the fact that this leaves me open to accusations of an 'England Centric' view of history. At which point I would point people to the subtitle of the book, and can only add that I may redress the balance with another book about Scotland one day. At the moment though, I am being as hypocritical with my choice of names for this war as the English media who refer to Andy Murray as British when he is winning and Scottish when he is losing! For people in Wales who think I might have forgotten you, let me just say the difference is that I have enjoyed visiting and touring in Wales – I've never yet even got around to going to Scotland!

Anyway, I was always told that one you're in a hole you should stop digging (although I've always worked more along the lines that once you've put your foot in it you might as well go up to the hip) so it is time to leave aside my poor attempts to avoid offending the other countries within the UK, and actually get down to a 'Condensed Histories' view of the reasons behind the English Civil War.

The first thing to say about the Civil War it that as a proportion of the population killed, it is the worst war on record for the people of the UK, killing a higher percentage of people in the UK than both World Wars. In fact, the adult male population was almost literally decimated[17]. At that point there was an estimated adult male population of two million people, of which about 84,800 are recorded as having been killed in fighting, with another 100,000 dying as a result of wounds or disease. The whole population of the UK at that time has been estimated at only about five million. So about 3.7% of the population of the UK died as a result of a war between the King and Parliament.

---

[17] In the word's original use, meaning the death of one in ten. The term originally comes from a Roman punishment for a mutinous Legion of soldiers, where one in ten of the soldiers in the Legion would be killed.

I know some of you saw a lot of numbers in the previous paragraph and skipped ahead to this one - and good for you in a way. Once you know that a lot of people died in the Civil War the actual figures aren't going to mean that much to you. Besides which you'll probably forget them very quickly indeed. If you read them then you probably already have in fact, and you are wondering whether I just added the figures into the book because I happened to know them and wanted to show off. If you were wondering that, you're half right. I also wanted to look thorough.

The important point is that between 1641 and January 30th 1649, a lot of people were killed in the wars between the army of the Parliament (Roundheads) and the King's army (Cavaliers). One of the people killed - on the latter date - was King Charles I who was 'executed', although as there was no legal basis for his trial at the time the word 'murdered' has also been used to describe the moment when his head was chopped off, although he was given a trial[18].

How had the country reached the point where the parliament and the King were at war with one another?

Partly it was, as was so often the case in the 16th and 17th centuries, about religious differences[19]. It was in a similar vein to old joke:

"Did you hear Mike's girlfriend left him? They had religious differences; she found God, and he found out it wasn't him"

Charles's belief that he was king by 'Divine Right' was displayed in far too much of an 'in your face' way for the parliament of the time, especially when they did have certain controls over him.

Then Charles really started to stir up trouble in the Catholic vs. Protestant feud which had been going on since Henry VIII had broken from the Catholic Church in Rome, with both

---

[18] As, of course, was Saddam Hussein. Sometimes the trial seems to be just a formality.]

[19] Aren't you glad we don't live in a world where religion triggers wars today…

denominations having spent some time as the illegal and persecuted religion in England, and keeping warm by being burned at the stake. He did this by marrying Henrietta Maria, a French Princess and Catholic; originally by proxy to speed things up, and avoid the protestant parliament of the time being able to stop the marriage.

While these issues of religion made Charles unpopular, there was still not enough there to warrant a rebellion against the King, which would be treason on a grand scale. There was also the far more pressing subject of money.

Charles was very short on money in the early part of his reign, and was limited to how he could raise more. He could not raise new taxes without the approval of parliament, and Queen Elizabeth had already sold off much of the land owned by the monarchy when she was in power to deal with her own financial problems.

So it was that, in complaint about Charles's marriage, along with other 'crimes' the parliament felt he was guilty of, Parliament drew up the 1628 Petition Of Right, essentially a list confirming that certain actions by the King, such as raising taxes without parliament, would be deemed illegal.

Charles took the parliament's petition and dealt with it in exactly the way you would expect an absolute monarch with a strong belief in divine right to do so – he dissolved parliament and ruled alone, without calling another parliament for the next 11 years, effectively creating a dictatorship with no challenge to his government.

As he couldn't raise taxes or create new taxes without recalling parliament, Charles came up with the clever but immoral 'work-around' of expanding 'ship-money'. This was a tax originally intended to apply to coastal towns in times of war, to fund the defence of the coast, and to ensure it was used correctly the towns could actually pay with ships! Charles extended this tax to inland towns in a time of (relative) peace in 1634. This tax was opposed at a lot of levels, but Charles managed to obtain signatures of ten out of twelve High Court judges to state that the King could levy this tax in 'times of danger', which were entirely at the King's discretion.

Eventually it was actual violent trouble in Charles's kingdom in Scotland (still a separate kingdom sharing a king) that led him to call a new parliament, after a series of riots and battles known as the 'Bishops' Wars' came about as a result of Charles introducing new reforms into the Scottish Church, changing it towards a High Anglican form of church, and in the view of many Scottish Presbyterians, dangerously close to Catholicism[20].

As soon as Charles recalled parliament in 1640, however, they were less interested in helping him and more interested in airing their grievances from the last eleven years, which led to this 'Short Parliament' being dissolved after just 3 weeks. This left Charles with no solution to the second Bishops' War, which was now underway, and was rapidly moving towards an all-out war between Scotland and England.

So come November 1640 Charles had to reconvene parliament again, and this time we have the 'Long Parliament', which would not be officially dissolved for another 20 years. They had Ship Money declared illegal in December, and managed fairly quickly to calm the troubles in Scotland, and begin negotiations, which went on until the 'Treaty of London' was signed in August 1641, by which time everybody had more trouble on their plates.

The parliament had organised the trial and execution of the Earl of Strafford, who had been a supporter of Charles, in May. By December of 1641 Parliament listed all of Charles's crimes and their complaints against him in a document known as the 'Grand Remonstrance'.

---

[20] The Bishop's Wars are a subject in themselves, and are well worth looking at until I get around to writing a book about Scotland. Any time you get the situation where a bishop in Brechin is taking services with loaded pistols within reach you know there is something interesting going on (although if your local bishop conducts services with a loaded pistol you may be wanting to call the police).]

This document passed through the House of Commons by only 11 votes, and Charles took this as a sign that he could now fight back against the parliament, and so he took soldiers down to the House of Commons and burst in to arrest the 5 leaders of the opposition. He soon found out they had been tipped off – and it became clear that Parliament now had control of London.

Charles left London for Nottingham, and once there he raised his banner, and at that point the war can be said to have begun.

There are a lot of changes to the English legal system which came about as a result of the Civil War, and the short lived republic which existed from the execution of Charles I until the return and crowning of Charles II in 1660, to stop one man ever taking the rule of the county again.

One of these, which without knowing this history may seem an odd law, is that the monarch cannot enter the House of Commons. The monarch's representative (known as 'Black Rod'), when going to summon the Commons to the House of Lords for the state opening of Parliament always has the door slammed in his face 3 times, to signify the right of the House Of Commons to question the right of the monarch's representative to enter, ever since Charles had entered in an attempt to arrest members of the house. A minor point of ceremony which actually has a deep symbolism behind it!

This chapter has actually been very focused and on track, and really close to being a chapter from a proper history book! Don't worry; normal service will be resumed shortly.

The Blitz Spirit
Did it really exist?

Earlier in the year I was leading some theatre workshops in the small (and beautiful) town of Monale in the north of Italy, a few miles outside of Turin, during which time there were some severe storms and winds bringing down trees and doing a fair amount of damage, including making the roof of our rehearsal room leak, and causing the poor bidella (caretaker of sorts) to perform a very entertaining dance with the school's only bucket!

One of the most impressive pieces of damage that I saw, in a lot of ways, was to an aeroplane that stands in the middle of a playground there, outside the window of the school.

It is an old Italian fighter plane, and looks impressive. And in the winds the canopy had been blown off of the cockpit and had smashed on the ground. This being a plane that had been designed to be aerodynamic it struck me as impressive that the wind had managed to do this damage.

When I first saw it, I was occupied with keeping the students away from the broken glass of the canopy and keeping them from getting hurt. By the time I got outside again to have a look for myself I was disappointed to find that the incredible efficiency of the council there meant that it had all been cleared up, and every piece of broken glass was gone.

I say disappointed because, although I was glad that the children could now go outside without being injured, I had wanted to take a small piece of the glass if I could. Not because I'm a kleptomaniac, but because I have listened for a long time to my Grandad's stories of collecting shrapnel as a child during the Blitz, and I wanted to be able to phone him and tell him that I had collected my own piece of shrapnel from an old fighter.

This incident got me thinking about the Blitz and the effects it had. Obviously the title of this chapter isn't meant to offend anyone who lost anybody in the Blitz– it was a terrible event that was just a small part of a brutal war, a war which brought about the deaths of millions of people across the globe.

From the 7th September 1940 until mid-May 1941 German bombs were dropped on London and other major cities throughout Britain in a series of frequent nightly raids, beginning with 57 nights of consecutive bombing in London. It is difficult now to imagine the scale of the bombings, but more than 40,000 civilians were killed over this period, and many buildings in London, Coventry and Plymouth, along with many other cities, were destroyed. In the first month alone over 5,000 tons of bombs were dropped on London alone, including both explosive and incendiary bombs. Overall no one can deny that this was a bad part of a very bad era in human history.

At this point, however, I have to go back to the subtitle of this chapter and point out a slight discrepancy between the statistics I have shown here, and the way the Blitz is often talked about, both generally and by those people I know who lived through it.

We refer a lot in this country to the 'Blitz Spirit'[21]. In a quick search of news stories just now I have found several results including an Evening Standard report that:

"An official inquiry into happiness in Britain has revealed a new "Blitz spirit" with a remarkably contented and calm nation getting on with life amid the gloomy headlines."

Also a headline from the Mail Online about the recession from a few years ago that tells us:

"The Blitz spirit will save us, insists Gordon Brown."

One more – a headline from The Independent talking about the rain at the Queen's jubilee:

---

[21] And when I say we, I don't think I have ever actually use the phrase except in a historical context, so I guess I mean the media.

"Diamond Jubilee: 'There was Blitz spirit; we were laughing in the face of adversity'"

Putting aside for a second the almost unbelievable lack of ability to judge the scale of tragedy that lets someone compare a rainy day to major bombing raids and loss of life, there is something more universal that comes out of this – the lasting impression of the Blitz as some sort of fantastic event which brought the people of London, and Britain as a whole, together; the idea that in the Blitz people followed the 'Keep calm and carry on' mentality, with sing-alongs in the air raid shelters.

This, along with my grandfather and other people from his generation who were children at the time who tell stories of shrapnel hunts, or like my Grandma who talks fondly of the time that she spent when she was evacuated from London as a child, leads in some ways to a very 'Dad's Army', watered down view of the Blitz… I think….

Looked at on paper there is no way people should be having any fond memories of the Blitz – the idea seems incredible. Yet out of this terrible period in history - in which the coming of the planes meant that civilians hundreds of miles away from the front lines were now being killed in vast numbers, and completely indiscriminately – we have a general feeling of warmth and pride.

Perhaps, and I'm perfectly willing to accept this if it is the case, I am the only person who has real trouble reconciling these two things. The pulling together for the greater good is one thing, but the fact that out of all of these events those which have sunk deepest into my consciousness from the Blitz is a sense of friendship and adventure, everybody getting together for a singsong while the city collapsed above them.

If I think of the trenches of the first war then I think first of the deaths of all the people, then of the heroism and stories of acts of kindness I have heard about the war. It is the same with the holocaust; the deaths are the first things to spring to mind, then the strength of the late Leon Greenman who I once heard talk about his time in Auschwitz. More recently the attacks on the Twin Towers in New York; when I think about that day my mind goes first to the images of death and destruction, and then to the stories of the bravery of the firemen, cops and others who were prepared to risk (and in some cases give up) their lives for the sake of others.

When I think 'Blitz', however, my mind goes first to the image of people in the underground stations sheltering together and singing, then to thoughts of 'Just William' style boys out looking for shrapnel. Bombs are nowhere near the top of the list of things I think of, down below rationing, sirens and spitfires.

Between the rose tinted memories and views of 'Blitz Spirit', and my thoughts that it seems almost unbelievable that people could have carried on normal lives and actually have fond memories during such events, there must, of course, lie the truth.

In the course of researching this chapter I have read one book which suggested the entire 'Blitz Spirit' thing is, if not a lie, then at least a misleading account of the events, and it made some compelling arguments.

The trouble I had though, was I found myself feeling a bit like the guy in the Matrix[22] when he is given the choice of taking a pill and going back to his happy life unaware that he is living in a virtual world created by machines, or take a pill which will allow him to leave that virtual world and face the horrors of a new world, but know the truth.

The idea of the British reaction to the Blitz has (and did almost immediately following the war) passed into the folklore of the nation. It has become a standard against which the country has begun to define itself; the British Bulldog, we're strongest when our backs are against the wall, keep carrying on idea that we would all like to see as a characteristic of the British people.

At that point in time I did something which I don't usually do. I put the book down and decided that it really wasn't for me. I actually found for all my saying that I couldn't believe that people could carry on and sing in the face of the Blitz that in fact I was wrong. The truth was that when it comes down to it I can't really

---

[22] A really current film reference there…

imagine people not doing that. What other choice did people have back then? Give up? All just spend their entire lives depressed and waiting for death?

Although I still believe that the phrase 'Blitz Spirit' is overused, and is inaccurate, I wouldn't want to live in a world where the idea behind it is wrong. I don't think it is, but at the same time I don't think it is something that the British people alone can be proud of. I personally think that it is one of the most powerful and endearing human traits that we, as a race, carry on. In the last fifteen years we have seen terrorist attacks, recession, wars, tsunami and hurricanes. If you look at all of these terrible events, no matter how bad, you will find stories of kindness and heroism, and above all you will find that people, on the whole, kept on going through the worst and as cities, nations, and as a race, survived.

For me, in a rare moment of love and fondness for the entire human race, I would like to say that perhaps what we call the 'Blitz Spirit' may really just be human spirit. If you want to research the history of the war and try and prove that there was no Blitz Spirit, or that death and destruction is the more important side of the Blitz than the survival, then feel free.

I am going, on this occasion, to listen to the majority of books I have read on the subject, and above all to listen to my Grandad when he tells me stories without bitterness. Perhaps it isn't the unbiased historian way to approach the subject, but sometimes I will just believe because Grandad says so.

Isabella de Fortibus
Queen of the Wight

Last week I found myself with a day free while the Ventnor Fringe Festival was on[23]. Having decided that this year wasn't the year to take on of my shows to the Edinburgh Festival because of budget restraints[24] I thought I could go along and support a local Fringe Festival and see what sort of work was being produced on the Island.

On arrival at just before four o'clock in the afternoon (don't ask what happened to the rest of the day) I found that the next show to be coming on was a one-man-comedy-musical which took place within the Spiritualist Church in Ventnor. It was a show with a lot of potential, and a very talented performer, but it was also one of the first performances and there was clearly a lot to be ironed out (and dropped entirely). I know the feeling! The first few performances of any of my shows always have pieces that seemed really funny to me in rehearsal, and after I've said them aloud to an audience they suddenly seem less funny!

Anyway, I'm straying off topic. In fact I haven't even really got on topic yet, which is a bad sign, as I thought this one was going to be a quick link in.

I watched the show, and halfway through there was a bustle of noise as a friend of mine and her daughter came into the room, breaking the atmosphere and disturbing the entire performance[25].

---

[23] By which I mean a day I should have spent researching for this book, but decided that it was a nice sunny day and I had something better to do! For those people who have real jobs and actual money - this is the best part of being a performer and writer.

[24] Or having no money. For people who have real jobs and actual money... I don't look so clever now!

[25] Not really, but she'll probably read this chapter and it will wind her up.

After the show was over, and as we exited, wondering whether we had actually enjoyed it or not (it was one of those kind of shows) we got to talking about other things, and I mentioned that I was doing a bit of writing about history, and she immediately said "Isabella de Fortibus".

Despite this seeming to me to be something of a non sequitur, it actually turns out that she was a person from the Isle of Wight's history that my friend told me I had to include in my book.

Now I don't want you to get the impression that I include things in this book just because somebody tells me too. She is, however, quite pretty, and I have a great deal of difficulty saying no to pretty girls (a difficulty which unfortunately they don't seem to reciprocate!). I therefore agreed to do a bit of research and put Isabella de Fortibus in the book if she was interesting enough[26], and she was - as you can probably tell from the fact that you are reading a chapter with her name at the top.

Once again I appear to have managed to fly way off topic before I even start on the subject the chapter is supposed to be about, so it's time to get on with some history!

Isabella de Fortibus was born Isabella de Revers in July 1237, the eldest daughter of the Earl of Devon at the time (who died in 1245, his title passing to Isabella's brother). She married young to William de Fortibus, Earl of Albemarle - and by young I mean very young. As in 'it would be illegal these days' young... as in 12. Although that was two years older than one of Isabella's daughters, Aveline, would be when she got married. It was clearly a very different time back then – however disturbing this may seem to us now!

 Unfortunately William died in 1260, when Isabella was just 23, although she was left some of his lands. The death of her husband was followed two years later by the death of her brother, and this

---

[26] Isabella, not my friend. My friend is not going in the book. Well, she sort of is in it now, but I'm not writing a chapter about her. Although so far she has had more page time than Isabella.

left her to inherit the title of Countess of Devon and Lady of the Wight (although many know her today as 'Queen of the Wight').

This is the point at which I found Isabella's place in history becoming really interesting. At first I thought that the titles meant that she was a local 'Lady' of the Isle of Wight as a local government representative to the King. However it turns out that this was a complete underestimation of the power she had on the Island, a power which went back to shortly after the Norman Conquest in 1066.

When Henry I gained the crown of England following the death of William II, he gave a number of titles to Richard de Redvers, including Lord of Devon. He was also granted the title of Lord of the Isle of Wight, although the Isle of Wight was given independently from England – the people of the Island owed their loyalty to Richard de Redvers rather than the King (although as Lord of Devon, de Redvers in turn owed his allegiance to the King).

This was passed down until it arrived at Isabella, who became the first and only Lady of the Wight with the powers, if not the official title, of a queen of the island. At that point in history the island was outside of the English Kingdom, a fact which no doubt makes all the born and bred islanders (which I am not, having been born and raised an Essex boy) very proud of once being independent from the 'mainland'.

As 'Queen of the Wight' it was only fitting that Isabella should live in a castle, and she had the beautiful Carisbrooke Castle sitting in the middle of the island. She even had the latest modern conveniences fitted – including glass windows[27]!

At least two men attempted to marry her and gain her wealth, but neither succeeded – although to avoid one she ended up hiding in a priory in Hampshire. I guess we've all got people we go to

---

[27] Which links us back to the Civil War – this is the castle where Charles was imprisoned for 14 months prior to his execution. His stay included an attempt to escape out of a window, which unfortunately failed because he had been so well cared for he was too fat and got stuck!

some lengths to avoid – for me it may well be my friend when she reads this chapter!

What I find really interesting, however, is what seems to be the very underhand way in which the Isle of Wight returned to the control of the King at the time of Isabella's death, in a series of circumstances which were suspicious to say the least. To clarify, it was the circumstances of Isabella's will and the passing of the island to the King that was suspicious, not her death itself. I would never dream of suggesting that the Royal Family would have a popular and powerful woman killed at any point in history…

Edward I had come to power in England in 1272, and had made no secret of the fact that he didn't want the island owned by anyone other than the King. In 1281 he had called Isabella to court and challenged her right to independent control over the island and its legal system, a challenge which she managed to defeat despite it taking place in the King's court.

He managed to confiscate some lands in 1284 from the Bishop of Winchester, covering five of the smaller towns and villages on the island, and at least twice attempted to buy the island from Isabella. Both offers were refused, the last time around Easter of 1293.

Isabella's health fell into decline that year, and on her way back from a visit to Canterbury she stopped at her house in Stockwell, where she lay terminally ill. The King immediately dispatched three bishops to 'persuade' her to sell her lands. From which point there are two different versions of the events of her final moments.

The first says that one of the bishops read a charter to her that made the sale to the king, and that Isabella agreed to it and had her maid seal it and confirm the deal. The second version, however, says that she touched the hand of one of the Bishops in her dying moments, and the King declared that this meant she had agreed to the sale.

Whichever version may be true, and with only the bishops and possibly the maid as witnesses we shall probably never know for sure, the island passed into the possession of the king, and was never again independently owned.

Isabella de Fortibus, however, proved herself a strong woman – strong enough to own and govern the Isle of Wight, strong enough to see off suitors, and strong enough to stop the King getting what he wanted.

I'm glad that my friend mentioned her to me at the Ventnor Fringe. Unfortunately when arrived to see some music at one of the performance areas after she had mentioned the 'Queen of the Wight' to me we were amazed to be told that unfortunately there was not going to be music as advertised at that point, because they had 'run out of buskers'. It wouldn't have happened in Isabella's day!

The Magna Carta
Signed at the bottom?

I'm going to talk about a joke. It is probably one of the oldest and least funny history related jokes I know – and if you've ever seen me perform live you will know I have a certain fondness for old and not very funny jokes. The trouble with some old jokes is that the things which they refer to have drifted out of common knowledge or common usage, and so the jokes no longer work.

Let me explain a little about one common way in which certain jokes work. A question is asked or a statement made which points towards a specific response. The answer, following statement or 'punch line' (as we say in the business) gives an unexpected response, and this surprise triggers laughter, or, as is more common in my shows, a groan. For example:

-   Where do you get virgin wool from?
-   Ugly sheep.[28]

You get the idea here. This joke may have inspired a wry smile from you, or at least a pitying shake of the head as you consider my comedy career going up in smoke. So how about this one:

-   Where was the Magna Carta signed?
-   At the bottom.

You probably get this joke too. If more than half of people reading this don't have a clue why that is funny (or supposed to be) then my readership isn't all that I have hoped for. However, according to a survey in 2008 carried out by 'YouGov' for the British library, 45% of the 2,073 people asked had no idea what the Magna Carta was, and of those who did know that it was a famous

---

[28] If you don't understand this, ask your parents. If you are an adult and you don't understand this, I feel sorry for you. If you're Welsh… aren't you glad I'm well above making any jokes about you!

charter, less than 32% of people knew that it limited the power of the monarch[29]. The one piece of information which I was less surprised that people did not realise, and in fact only 19% of people did, was that the charter only applies to England, not the whole UK, coming long before there was a single kingdom, and even hundreds of years before one King ruled the UK as multiple kingdoms. Congratulations if you did.

The article I read which first pointed this survey out to me, and led me to look deeper into the survey, was making the point of what a terrible thing it was that people had so little knowledge of the Magna Carta, (or 'Great Charter' as it translates – a fact which escaped David Cameron when he was asked in an interview on American television) as it is the fundamental basis of our freedoms and rights, and read to me as if the writer intended to suggest that there was some way in which not knowing this made people in some way stupid. To me, personally, the greatest loss in this is that it means 45% of people wouldn't have a clue what the old joke about the Magna Carta meant, so they would just look at me confused or bored rather than even moaning that it was a bad joke.

It does raise a question though – how important is it that people should know about the Magna Carta, and the details of what it contains? I think I may be stepping out of line with a lot of historians (or historians of a certain ilk) and a lot of people who complain about 'dumbing down' when I say that I don't think it is actually such a major thing for people to know. Obviously I would like more people to have an interest in the Magna Carta and in history, which is why I have included it in my book. If they don't know about a charter from 1215 though, is it going to upset their life? At least 45% of people would probably say no.

I had this discussion with a friend of mine a few years back who said I was being an idiot - the line of reasoning a lot of people seem to take when arguing with me - and that people should know

---

[29] And I'm not a supporter of surveys generally because you can get a survey to prove pretty much anything if you want. I have done a rough check among the people I've run into today though, and this does seem fairly accurate!

about the Magna Carta because it was 'like an English constitution', and it 'stops the monarch seizing power over us today' and 'protects our rights'. At this point, I confess, I may have openly laughed in his face. There is nothing that will make me laugh quicker than somebody hypocritically claiming that people should know all about something, and then showing their own ignorance on the subject[30].

He was picturing the Magna Carta in the same way that I have found many people I have talked to about this do, as a similar document to the American Constitution – which is a document which I do think that any American should know, and I have found that most do. That is because the American Constitution is a clear set of rules about the way the USA should be governed, and the rights of the US citizens. It is also, importantly, aside from a few amendments (most famously the Bill of Rights) still current in legislation today.

The Magna Carta is certainly not a constitution. We do not have any specific written constitution – any 'constitution' of England would have to be taken as the sum of many, many documents and laws. The Magna Carta is a document which King John was forced to sign after a rebellion against his 'tyranny'. In signing the document, which contained 63 clauses, King John limited his powers, including ensuring the Church was free of royal interference, that the King could not pass taxes without consent of Parliament, and the right of every person not to be held without the 'lawful judgement by his equals or by the law of the land'. This was an agreement and a list of laws, but was not a constitution.

Nor, in fact, does the document as a whole continue to have any power, and in fact of the 63 clauses only 3 still remain valid, the other 60 were either removed from subsequent copies of the charter, are redundant, of have been repealed, according to the British Library website.

---

[30] One of the main reasons why I try never to claim that people 'should' know about anything - other than classic comedy series like Dad's Army, Monty Python or The Goon Show.

Of the three that the library lists as still 'valid', I would have to question the continued validity of at least two. The first is that the Church should be free from interference from the King. As since then we have had the dissolution of the monarchies, the executions of both Catholics and Protestants as different Tudor and Stewart monarchs changed the official religion back and forth, and as the monarch is now head of the Church of England. How something can be seen to be free from influence from its own governor I'm not quite sure.

The second clause that the British Library still sees as valid, however, is far more important in my views. It is:

"No free man shall be seized or imprisoned, or stripped of his rights or possessions, or outlawed or exiled. Nor will we proceed with force against him except by the lawful judgement of his equals or by the law of the land. To no one will we sell, to no one deny or delay right or justice."

It galls me to say it, but I do fear that even this oldest fundamental principle, the one part of the Magna Carta which makes it really worth knowing about, as it contains the basis of our right to a fair trial and to be treated as 'innocent until proven guilty', no longer seems to be valid thanks to the Terrorism Act in 2006, which brought the amount of time a person could be held without charge up to 28 days, with many politicians pushing for 90 days. 28 days, held, without charge, whatever the reason, sounds to me like a free man is being seized and imprisoned without the judgement of his equals, and that justice is certainly being delayed for innocent people held under this law[31].

So is it important that people know the exact date that the Magna Carta was signed, where it was signed, or what all of the outdated provisions in it were? It would certainly be nice if people knew about this and where the basis of some of their rights and our political system and freedom from tyranny came from.

---

[31] Although according to the Home Office website today, the maximum time you can currently be held without charge under the latest anti-terrorism laws is back to 14 days. Still too long in my opinion.

Personally, though, I can live without people knowing these things, as long as they are making sure that they keep an eye on the present and the future to ensure we hold on to our rights and stay free from tyranny and oppression. Knowing your history is important in this respect, especially now. Knowing how many times people have used a threat from outside, such as the threat of terrorism the country has felt since the attacks of 9/11 and the 7th July 2005, as an excuse to slowly chip away at the rights which people have fought for over hundreds of years is, in my view, more important than remembering the details of one outdated charter which began to outline some of the rights which we should expect.

For those of you still wondering where the King John signed the Magna Carta, he didn't. He would have put his seal on it – because there is in fact no evidence that King John could write! Maybe we're not dumbing down so much after all.

For the record, the 'exam answer' to the question would be Runnymede - although there is no evidence that a charter was actually written up and signed at the meeting there that day, even though the terms were agreed there. It was probably drawn up afterwards and where the King actually was when he put his seal on each of the copies of the charter can't be known for certain.

Jack the Ripper
Sex and Violence!

I understand that some historical subjects can be a bit dry – and the signing of an ancient charter like that in the last chapter is hardly going to inspire excitement, especially when I conclude that it isn't vital to know about it. So now I'm going to talk about the dark Whitechapel streets, prostitutes, and murder. Bet you're focussed now![32]

The trouble with this chapter is with what exactly to write on such a well-known subject. I'm going to be writing about things that some people think they know, and which other people disagree with, and show how little we are actually sure of. The whole 'Jack the Ripper' story has been investigated so many times, by so many people. It has appeared in so many books and films and with so many contradictions, that not only do we not know who 'Jack the Ripper' was, but we also lack for certain other pieces of information. For example:

- How many people did he kill?
- Did he actually send any notes to the police?
- Was he upper or lower class?
- Why did he do it?
- Was 'he' a 'he'?
- Above all – was he just a media construct? Was one person responsible for a number of murders or were these separate murders clumped together to make a good story?

---

[32] I'm hoping that the whole 'videogames cause violence' thing doesn't work with books. If you're likely to be suggestible enough to go out and kill prostitutes after reading a chapter like this, then please stop reading now! - I wouldn't want that on my conscience.

I imagine some of you are about to argue with some of my points – either because you are certain that the case was solved because you read a book, or because you saw a film with Johnny Depp in it where he solved it. However no matter how good an actor Johnny Depp may be, this doesn't actually count as conclusive proof of anything. I think, however, that most people know that there are a range of possible suspects in the 'Ripper' cases, and most 'ripperologists'[33] will have their personal favourites.

I'm not even any more interested in the Ripper that I am in most areas of history, but even I have my favourite suspect, Charles Cross. He was a cart driver who supposedly found the first victim, and was kneeling over her when the next person arrived on the scene. Recent theories have suggested that he had actually just killed the woman and when he was caught in the act pretended he had just found the body. He isn't my favourite suspect because I think that he is the most likely candidate – I don't – but because it conjures up a darkly comic scene in my mind where, like a husband caught in bed with another woman, this man kneeling there cutting open a corpse comes up with a barely plausible excuse for his presence - and is believed.

I'm not about to attempt to solve the case in this chapter – people have spent many years and a lot of work in investigating the case and have not come up with a definitive answer, and I don't want to show them up by solving the entire case in one chapter of the book – especially as I'm not even entirely sure that the series of murders which most people see as Jack's crimes can be attributed to the same person.

I am just going to use this chapter to raise doubt about the number of women who were actually killed by the serial killer known as 'Jack the Ripper', because this is one of the facts that I

---

[33] Oh, yes, 'ripperologists' is a word. And I'm amazed that more of them aren't rounded up each time there is a murder in London. I'm not saying all ripperologists are serial killers, of course. In the same way that I don't think that every person that works in a shoe shop has a foot fetish – but you can't deny there must be some…

though was pretty certain before I started looking in to Jack's history for a short article I was writing about a Neolithic monument, for a local paper on the Isle of Wight earlier this year. If you are wondering why I was looking into Jack the Ripper to write about a Neolithic monument on the Isle of Wight, you really must be struggling with some of the other connections in this book!

The obvious answer to the number of victims, and the most common answer, is 5, although the 'Whitechapel Murders' in the official police files cover eleven unexplained deaths from April 1888 to February 1891 in Whitechapel. In ripperology there are what are known as the 'canonical' victims, those that are generally held as the definitive victims of Jack The Ripper (in much the same way that there are 'canonical' stories in comic books, or the 'canonical' Bond films, which don't include the original 'Casino Royale' or 'Never Say Never Again' – despite the fact that 'Never Say Never Again' starred the definitive Bond. No arguments.). These five victims are:

Mary Anne Nichols

Annie Chapman

Elizabeth Stride

Catherine Eddows

Mary Jane Kelley

Of these I imagine that if you have heard of only one it will be Mary Kelly; arguably the most famous 'Ripper' victim - and I would argue with it because I would have to argue with the idea of her being a Ripper victim at all, or maybe even with the idea of Mary Kelly being a murder victim at all[34].

I won't go into the gory details of all of these murders – you may be reading this book over breakfast and I wouldn't want to be

---

[34] Not, I hasten to add, that I think it was possibly suicide. Nobody, not even Jonathan Creek, could devise a way for the type of wounds inflicted on her to have been done by her own hand. The question asked is whether the body was that of Mary Kelly at all.

responsible for you bringing your breakfast back up all over it, although I will touch on some of the details as we go through, because otherwise some people will feel I've cheated them out of a bit of Jack the Ripper gore and violence. As I'm going to try and point out that there was probably more than one killer, I might as well bring some of the differences between the death of Mary Kelly and those of the other canonical victims first – although I'm not even convinced that the other four were killed by the same hand.

If this wasn't a Condensed History I'd go into Liz Stride in more detail as well – and I suggest if you are interested that you do.[35] Just making the case against Mary Kelly being a victim of the same killer will be enough to demonstrate that even the generally accepted 'facts' of the case are still open to a lot of dispute.

The first difference is in age. Mary was 25 when she died, while the other four canonical victims were all in their mid-forties, and she is often held as being far more attractive than the others – probably true because poor, street-walking prostitutes in that part of London in that era are unlikely to have aged very well at all. She was also in slightly better circumstances than the others, because she owned her own residence. This meant that while the others had to stay in temporary accommodation when they had the money, and were forced to carry out their 'business' on the streets themselves, Mary could take her 'customers' back to her house to… I'm really starting to run out of euphemisms already. So there were clear differences in the age and lifestyle to differentiate her from the other victims - arguably subtle differences, but enough to raise questions.

All of which having been said, I hope that you have now finished your breakfast, or anything else that you might have been eating earlier in the chapter, because things are going to take a slide towards the gruesome, and I'm not going to pull any punches, I've

---

[35] While I am not generally referencing in this series of books, I would like to make special mention to 'Saucy Jack' in Paul Woods and Gavin Baddeley's fantastic 'Devil's Histories' series of books as being worth a read if you want to know more about the Ripper.

talked about documents and monuments and archaeologists, but now I get to have a go at some real descriptive horror writing as we get on to the differences in the murders themselves.

The first four victims in the canon were all killed in the streets; Mary on the other hand was killed indoors. This difference can obviously be explained away by the fact that she had a place to go indoors, and that she worked indoors, and so was less likely to be on the streets at that time of night. This just makes the two differences of the type of person and the type of location of the murder into one big difference, it doesn't serve to explain the change in 'Jack's' pattern if they were all killed by one person.

Then we move on to the level of violence in the attack on Mary Kelly. It was beyond that seen in any of the previous attacks, and may have implanted itself, more than any of the other scenes, on the minds of ripperologists and members of the public today, because it was one of the first crime scenes where forensic photography was in use. She was the only victim who was photographed in situ, photographs which, once seen, are hard to forget – and this from someone who is supposed to have been desensitised to violence thanks to films and violent video games.

The other bodies had all been found with the throats cut, and all bar Stride had cuts to the abdomen – and as Stride was the first of two in a night it has been suggested that she either wasn't a victim of 'Jack', or that he may have been disturbed. On two occasions, the second and forth canonical victims, the uterus was removed, and in the fourth victim part of the left kidney was also taken.

These wounds seem horrible and severe, but compared to the wounds on Mary they seem simple. Her throat had been cut, as with the others, and the uterus and both kidneys removed, but that was just the start. The breasts were cut off, and everything covering the abdomen and thighs were also sliced off. The uterus, kidneys and one breast were found under her head, and the other contents of the abdomen were removed and scattered around the body, with the body itself seemingly carefully arranged and laid out. There was blood on the walls and in a pool on the floor. This could all be seen as escalation of the killer's attacks on the abdomens of the other women. However in the case of Mary her face was also mutilated, her nose almost sliced off, and her ears and cheeks also deeply cut. Her lips and arms had been sliced. She would later be identified by her boyfriend only by her ears and eyes as the rest of her face was too messed up, giving rise to some theories that it wasn't Mary Kelly at all.

If I am honest, when I set out to write this chapter I was quite excited at the prospect of being able to describe a 'Ripper' mutilation, it was going to be something different from the sort of descriptions I usually write in history and in other works I do. I must admit though, that having spent an afternoon going over different descriptions, including the Doctor's report which made the basis for most of my description, and picking out the salient points, as well as having another look at photographs of the body, that as I wrote this I felt quite ill. No hyperbole; literally, physically, I felt sick. I've just looked into a mirror and seen that I am looking quite pale, and I'm not surprised. I don't expect you'll feel close to this just reading this description, but I hope you felt a passing moment.

I am going to push on though, and continue the chapter rather than taking a break to let myself settle a little, because we are nearing the end of what I am going to say about the 'Ripper' and his murders.

I think you can see from this why there is doubt that the same serial killer murdered all five of these women, It was a big escalation in violence and a different type of victim for the last attack, and to include all of these women means casting a slightly wider net on the type of murders that this man would have committed.

If there was one man who had killed all these women, why did he stop with Mary Kelly– or did he? Did he start with Mary Ann Nichols? If we accept the disparities in these attacks and maintain the idea they were committed by one killer, then we must consider Martha Tabram as a possible first victim, a prostitute in her late thirties, killed in the start of August 1888, less than a month before

Nichols. She was stabbed thirty-nine times, with wounds from her neck to her abdomen – key areas in the Ripper's attacks on at least three of the canonical victims (not counting Stride whose abdomen was untouched, and Kelly, where little was left untouched).

There are also 4 more murders in the 'Whitechapel' file after Mary Kelly, including two who had their throats cut and one who was found only as a headless and legless torso.

From all of this evidence it is easy to see why there is confusion about the number of people killed by 'Jack the Ripper', if indeed they were serial murders carried out by the same person, and not copycat killings. If you accept all of the canonical victims, then why not assume he began with a frenzied attack on Tabram, when her attacker focused on the same areas of the body, and she fit his victim profile better than Kelly.

Or to look at it another way, if we accept that there were a number of killers killing prostitutes in Whitechapel in this period, many of them with a tendency to attack the throat and mutilate, then why assume that the very different crimes included in the canonical five are all committed by the same person.

I said at the outset that I wasn't going to aim to solve the mystery in this chapter, and I haven't even begun to detail all of the mysteries surrounding the case, let alone come to a solution. I think this will always be one of the dark mysteries of England's past, and a solution which satisfies everyone and would hold up in a court of law will probably never be found.

I have, however, learned one important fact. That in a house alone, at night, in the dark midwinter, is not the best time or place to finish writing a chapter about such a dark subject. I'm going to stop writing now, and go and double check the doors… again…

The Hundred Years War
Before counting was popular

There are many things in this world where the name can be a little misleading. Koala Bears, for example, are marsupials, not bears. Your 'funny bone' is a nerve, the lead in your pencil[36] is not made of lead and shooting stars are not stars. This leads us on to the Hundred Years War.

The Hundred Years War between England and France started in 1337. I'm going to admit that I spent most of my A-level maths lessons down the pub with my friends instead of the classroom, although it wasn't really my fault – one of them was on a Friday afternoon and I couldn't really make it back after a lunchtime of drinking and pool. Despite this, even I am fairly confident that 1337 add 100 would see the war ending in 1437. It didn't. It actually finished in 1453, and so it lasted at least 116 years.

Some of you may now be questioning my maths skills even more when I use the words 'at least' 116 years, as though mathematics isn't an exact science, which it more or less is. What isn't an exact science however is history, which begins to explain why we get the name of 'The Hundred Years War' given to a war that lasted more than a hundred years. The trouble is that historians like to label things, and these labels don't necessarily fit - and sometimes try to make things a little more convenient than they were.

For a start the 'Hundred Years War' was not even a period of continuous fighting – there were periods of peace in between – and there was fighting with France before this period and after. Yet the label sticks and covers a particular period of war between the two countries, covering the period from Edward III of

---

[36] *Not a euphemism!* Behave.

England claiming that he was also the true King of France, until the final (for the moment) defeat of the English army at the Battle of Castillion on the 17th July 1453. Of course we'll be glossing over the final result a bit here…

So having taken the time to completely destroy the naming of the 'Hundred Years War', let's put that to one side and actually look at the 'war' itself. Why it happened and why we completely smashed the French at the Battle of Agincourt.

The why is simple – it was all about who ruled France. It must have been a simpler time when you could actually go to war and state as your aim from the outset that you were doing it to control a region. Certainly there is no suggestion that Edward III declared war on France because he suspected them of having some sort of 'crossbow of mass destruction' hidden from weapons inspectors. Instead he declared himself the rightful King of France, based party on the fact that he was the nephew of King Charles IV of France who had died in 1327, and whose other nephew had become King Philip VI of France, partly on the fact that Philip had been trying to regain parts of France that England still owned (having at one time owned half of France), and partly on the fact that Philip had been supplying weapons to the Scots[37]. That is basically the why of the war – a much simpler question to answer when it came down to monarchs and their greed, than today when even a summary of the causes behind the First World War could easily fill an entire book.

I would love to go on and claim victory in the war for the English – as an Englishman I am only too well aware of the friendly feud that exists between the English and the French when it comes to discussion of our past wars. I worked on a French ship for some months as an entertainer, with all of the crew outside of the entertainment staff being French, and I got used to being referred to as 'Roast Beef'. Ironic considering that they never really managed to properly cook my beef the way I like it in the galley, no matter how many times I offended the chef by asking him to completely burn it.

---

[37] Although not weapons of mass destruction, obviously.

The fact of the matter, though, is that we went into the war with a small amount of property in the north of France, and Gascony in the south, and came out of it owning nothing more than Calais – which was probably blocked up half the time anyway with cart driver strikes. I think that it is safe to say, overall, that we definitely lost the war.

This is why when talking about the Hundred Years War there is a tendency amongst the more patriotic of the English to gloss over the final result and to instead discuss the Battle of Agincourt in 1415. It is sort of like a football fan, who has just watched a humiliating defeat of his team, ignoring the final result to talk about the skill of one goal scored by his team – as opposed to the 5 by the other team. I think this analogy probably works, but I'm not actually completely sure, because I know next to nothing about football.

Anyway, being of that nature of Englishman who will mention the 1966 World Cup and ignore the fact England hasn't won since (and that I probably wouldn't notice if we did), I will of course be focussing now on the Battle of Agincourt as well, because that was a day on which we definitely won. The main reason for this is that we took English Longbows, along with English Archers[38].

If you think that using superior weaponry doesn't sound like it lives up to the famous English ideals of 'fair play', then you are probably right, but seem to have forgotten the 19th Century habit in the British Empire of having battles against people who were armed with spears while the British army were equipped with guns and canons – remember Michael Caine in Zulu?. There has always been a slight grey area in the rules of fair play when it comes to war, much as it is respected to an insane amount at other points in war.

In fact, before the end of the battle, worse would be to come as Henry V - the King of England by this point - ordered the killing of all the French prisoners taken by that point. It was considered a

---

[38] Yes, ok, and Welsh archers, who were for the sake of argument every bit as good as the English archers. Well done the Welsh!

justified move, even by those French reporters on the battle, owing to the fact that Henry could not contain so many prisoners and was fearful of another wave of attacks by the remaining French Army. On the other hand, it was hardly cricket.

Now winning a battle may not seem an important enough victory to hold on to – but one of the main reasons it is such a remembered victory in England is the fact that by all rights the French should have won. The English army, numbering around six thousand men, were hungry and tired following a seventeen day march, much of it in the rain, and with much of the army suffering with dysentery[39], and trying to avoid battle with the French army, which now stood somewhere between twenty and thirty thousand men.

The position of the battle was important, as was one fact about the English army that it seems likely the French did not know at the outset. Of the six thousand men under the twenty-eight year old Henry's command, approximately five thousand were longbow men – more than would have been expected. Hesitation from the French army, who didn't want to charge into them, knowing full well the danger of being the attacking army when bows were involved, allowed the English army to move into a position a little over three hundred yards from the French army, and crucially into a position where the English army now ran to the edge of a wood on both sides.

The usual approach on an open battlefield to combat archers would be to use the cavalry to try and outflank them – to get around the side or behind the archers and therefore avoid a head on charge into a hail of arrows. With the English lines tight against the woods this wasn't an option, and the ground between the armies was soft and hard to traverse.

The English started firing small numbers of arrows into the French army - the distance of the best longbows giving them this

---

[39] If you don't know what dysentery is, I suggest you look it up on the internet. I've only just recovered after the Jack the Ripper chapter; I don't need to be talking about any bum related diseases right now.

option. At this point the French gathered a hasty cavalry charge, and in the study of battles it is usually found that a hasty response to enemy provocation is not a good move; and so it proved in this case. It wasn't even the full strength of cavalry that charged, and muddy ground slowed them down as arrows rained into them. From here on in, although not a foregone conclusion, the English had their chance to win, and having chosen their battleground, and provoked the French into a hasty charge, the English had the upper hand.

From here on in the battle largely went the way of the English, and the killing of prisoners was a tough decision to make, but in the context of the times and battle was justified. Had Henry not given the order to kill the prisoners when he did, many of whom were still at least partially armed; the day could well still have been lost.

This, therefore, is the battle that the English tend to choose to remember when talk about the Hundred Years War, the French less so.

It is important, however, when we look back on history to ensure that any 'friendly rivalries' between nations remain exactly that – friendly. I have mentioned my time on the French boats and the comments that were passed in good taste between the English and the French staff. Never any malice behind them, and if there had been it would, I'm sure, have stopped – mainly because we were outnumbered much of the time by about a hundred to one, even worse odds than the battle.

So when I write about Agincourt and the victory of the English or we make jokes about it and bring it up repeatedly over dinner with a French crew, it is important also to respect and remember the honour and bravery of the soldiers on both sides. This isn't a comment just on this battle, or this war either. When I watch a war film and see Richard Attenborough outsmarting the Nazi captors in 'The Great Escape', or cheer the success of the bouncing bombs in 'Dambusters', I enjoy feeling proud of the English for our part in winning this war, and I think that this is a good thing, to feel proud of the men who fought and died for us. As long as it never spills over into feeling anything but respect for the other countries involved, and above all, as someone smarter than I wrote, for "the soldiers of all nations who lie killed".

Charles Darwin
The pinnacle of evolution?

We don't always end up entirely where we expect in life. About a decade ago when I finished my A-levels and went out to face the big wide world[40] I was very clear that I was going to be a 'serious actor'. Not just any type of actor, but a Shakespearean actor, and I was going to perform with the Royal Shakespeare Company one day. My absolute acting hero at the time was Patrick Stewart (which hasn't changed in the least) – I once went to see him perform in David Mamet's 'A Life in Theatre' with my family when I was quite ill, because I couldn't stand to miss the chance to see him perform! I was hallucinating and feverish all the following night and day, but I'm glad I went because it was one of the best performances I have ever seen! I was going to work on my voice until I could achieve that same old school Shakespearean gravitas to my performances as him.

After a decade out in the 'real world' - or as close to it as I have ever reached - I can't believe I ever wanted that. I still love the works of Shakespeare and the RSC, but the idea of speaking the same lines without variation night after night feels me with dread. The plays I have performed over the last ten years have all had elements of improvisation and play, and now as an escapologist, comedy performer and in my writing I have left the routine behind, trying to avoid anything more than a vague structure to the words in my shows and flying off on tangents and improvisations wherever possible.

So my life hasn't quite gone the way I expected a few years ago, which I suppose is true of most of us. However I don't think many people have seen their lives move as far as Charles Darwin; from

---

[40] My degree came from the Open University – I was never interested in another 3 years of institutionalisation.

his intended life course when he started out in university of becoming a clergyman, to becoming the man who made famous the Theory of Evolution, and who through his publication of 'On The Origin Of Species' would create headaches for the church worldwide – and is still causing headaches in parts of the world today where there are still arguments about whether evolution should be taught in schools, or whether 'creationism'[41] should be taught as well.

It was only in 2008 that the Church of England made a formal apology to Darwin for suggesting he was wrong – much in the same way that in 2000 the Pope apologised for putting Galileo on trial for daring to suggest the Earth moves around the Sun, rather than the other way around, as the Bible states, only three hundred and fifty-eight years too late to affect Galileo's life.

So my subject for this chapter isn't evolution itself, or even the details of the response to his work and the controversy it created – it will be far more fun to look at that when the series takes me to the United States and I can get to grips with the Scopes Monkey Trial in Tennessee, which really is one of the most fascinating points in the whole 'debate', but happened too far out of England and without the direct involvement of Darwin, so even with my flexible approach to my own rules I can't shoehorn it in here.

My subject is rather how this man made the move in his life from wannabe clergyman, to being one of the names most associated with challenging the knowledge of the Church. Although he never claimed to be an atheist, he professed himself as an Agnostic, and would go for walks outside while his family was in Church from the time he was forty, ten years before 'On The Origin Of Species' was actually published. Both prominent atheists, such a Richard Dawkins, and some creationists and fundamentalist Christians, however, have claimed that Darwin was a fully-fledged atheist, for their own reasons.

----

[41] You know… the world is 6000 years old, dinosaur fossils are some sort of clever trick played on man by a god who apparently likes the odd practical joke. Not backed up by any actual evidence (how could it be)… Can you tell where I stand on Creationism yet?

In my mind it is up for a person themself to state their religion, and so the furthest we can say is that Darwin was at least agnostic – he no longer believed there was a god; although neither did he firmly state that he thought there was no god. For my purposes it isn't important either, because whichever way you look at it, it is a big step from clergyman.

The real truth is that to boil it down to one moment where Darwin suddenly decided that a literal belief in the Bible, and the certainty that there was a God is, as with all things in both life and especially in history, far too simplistic. A lot of people refer to his boarding the Beagle, the ship on which he voyaged for nearly five years from December 1837, as the turning point, because he decided to delay becoming a clergyman, instead choosing to travel on the Beagle and work as a naturalist on board the ship. There is the suggestion made that he was looking as he set out to discover evolution, although this obviously wasn't the case.

When Darwin set out on the Beagle we know he was still religious, he is reported to have quoted the Bible on moral questions, and set out through nature to prove intelligent design in the universe by looking to understand how the set of animals that God had created had spread throughout the world, rather than looking for a contrary explanation.

By the time he got off the boat at the end of the Voyage, however, he had begun to doubt a literal translation of the Bible. Partly this was due to his reading of works by scientists such as Charles Lyell a geologist whose work promoted and developed the idea of 'Uniformitarianism', which is the theory that the geological processes still at work today were responsible for the formation of the Earth's surface – and was at odds to the idea of Noah's flood and other immediate events as depicted in the Old Testament. He also had a number of questions rising from some of the finds he had made on his voyage. One of these was the discovery of fossil bones in Patagonia of recently extinct species which appeared to have died out without a trace of any form of major catastrophe or change to the local conditions. He also had questions as a result of discovering some species including mockingbirds in the Galapagos

Islands, which were found to have subtle differences from island to island.

Once back in England, Darwin would begin to try and construct a theory to explain all of the things he had noted and questioned on the voyage, and fresh information that was coming in as the specimens he had returned to England with were studied, and he began to investigate farmers' and breeders' techniques to breed specific qualities into animals and plants. From this he began to form a theory of animals developing over time, and by 1842 he was confident enough to send out his ideas of 'natural selection' to a number of friends. However in this work, although he discussed natural selection, he crucially included in his conclusion the sentence:

"It accords better with the lowness of our faculties to suppose each must require the fiat of a creator, but in the same proportion the existence of such laws should exalt our notion of the power of the omniscient Creator."

In other words he was arguing that the process of natural selection and evolution which he was discovering and which was contrary to the ideas in Genesis, (the Bible book - not the band) that God had created all of the animal species in one day, did not rule out the existence of God. He is saying that a truly powerful God would create a world with a set of rules to allow the animals to adapt and grow – an important philosophical concept which many Christians use today to reconcile the evidence and fact of evolution with their beliefs.

Darwin kept his theory under wraps, wanting to make sure that it was as watertight as possible before he released it, because he knew it would create controversy and damage to the Church. It was in 1849 that he stopped attending Church, and only ten years after that, when he heard that someone was going to release a paper on similar subjects, that Darwin published his 'On the Origin of Species' first.

This first announced to the world his twin ideas that there are inheritable differences between individuals within a species, and that these genes will only be passed on, through natural selection, by those members of any species who are more successful at surviving, thus leading to the evolution of species. Any mention of a god being involved in this process was left out of this book and Darwin's move from a man intending to become a clergyman, to the man who is one of the symbols of science over religion was complete.

Now it is time for me to summarise this into a deep point, and I have been debating throughout the writing of this chapter exactly which of two points I want to conclude the chapter with. The first would be a point about tolerance, about religious and scientific minded people being able to live together, but I don't think that is the point that I am looking to make.

I think the important thing here is about change. In my own life I could have stuck to my guns – at first when I realised I was drifting towards comedy I thought this might be giving something up, giving up my high ideals of being a 'serious actor'. It took me a little while to realise that I had more fun and was better being a more comical and light-hearted performer, and that I was never going to be Patrick Stewart, and would never really want to be[42]. I don't claim to have gone through the same level of change as Darwin, although in other areas of my life I have also made similar changes of my thoughts and opinions.

This then is the point I want to make at the end of this chapter, and it is simple, but not easy. You have a right to believe whatever you choose to believe of course, and to think whatever you want to think in this world. I would just urge everybody to investigate the world, to try to learn the truth, and if you reach that difficult point where your beliefs are challenged by the facts and evidence, to at least consider the evidence and consider the possibility that you are wrong. I don't want to make this specific about religion or evolution, I mean in everything. If you come from a background with racist beliefs, sexist beliefs, or any other beliefs, consider the evidence of your own life. It is the way to avoid prejudice, and the

---

[42] I respect the great man too much to make a comment about having to give up my beautiful hair!

most sensible way to respond to an argument, even if it is usually the most difficult.

And if you discover that instead of being the kind of performer who gains a great deal of respect by performing the works of the bard, you are better off as the type of performer who gets chained up in a sack while a steamroller drives at you, then roll with it, and you'll probably find you're better off if you don't try to stay stuck with ideas you can no longer justify.

Elizabethan Witches
No stakes please, we're British.

In 1935, Hitler stirred up fear that Jews were undermining German society, and in the Third Reich the Nuremberg Laws were passed, severely limiting the rights of Jews within the country, and making them not even second class citizens within the country, but specifically refusing to accept that any Jew could be a citizen of the Reich, and taking away their right to vote. This led ultimately to the Holocaust, to systematic murder and genocide.

On February 9th 1950 Joseph McCarthy stirred up fear that there were Cold War traitors within the US government, when he gave a speech in West Virginia during which he produced a list of 'known Communists' working within the State Department of the USA. This led to the hunting down, accusing and imprisonment of people in various walks of US life, many with little, or inconclusive, evidence of involvement in any way of being 'traitors', purely because they were accused of involvement with a political movement.

Following the fear of terrorism in the wake of the September 11th bombings in New York, many anti-terrorism laws were passed within the UK. Along with the changes in law was a change in policy for the armed police in the country for confronting terrorist suspects, known as Operation Kratos. This included the advice that the head of a suspected suicide bomber should be the target of shots when it seems that the bomber has no intention of surrendering. This policy has led to the death of at least one innocent man, Jean Charles de Menezes in Stockwell Tube Station in 2005, just two weeks after the London bombings of 7th July.

A culture of fear, misunderstanding, prejudice, and intolerance all have their roles to play in these horrific events from history – including recent history. What is sad is that certain lessons in history never seem to be learned, and instead the same events are repeated over and over.

When Arthur Miller came to write his play, The Crucible, he wanted to speak out against McCarthy's actions in America, but knew he couldn't directly attack without becoming a victim himself. Instead he wrote about the Salem Witch Trials of the 1600s, and cleverly showed the link between the two events to anyone who cared to look for it. I don't claim to be as clever as Arthur Miller, or as subtle – so I have started this chapter by blatantly pointing out the similarity that exists between the events mentioned above, and the response to Witchcraft in Elizabethan England.

The one fact that I think it is important to bear in mind, is the number of people who were burned at the stake for being witches in Elizabethan England, and I went in search of the highest estimate to include in this chapter, because it is the iconic image that I envision when I think of Witch Trials, the image of burning the Witch. The number, however, is slightly smaller than I expected. The number is 0.

Before you begin to think that this has slightly undermined my connection with some of the horrific events above, I would also like to point out that this is just because in England that this was not the method of execution chosen for witches, mainly I think because it was reserved largely for Catholics[43].

Some of you, who have been reading some of the light hearted comments in this book – I shy away from the word funny because, let's face it, they probably aren't – you may be wondering about my choice to start this chapter with talk of events including the horrors of the Holocaust, McCarthyism, and September 11th before I launch into my first comment mentioning Blackadder. No doubt some people will read this and tut or shake their heads that I should callously use such events to try and add some gravitas to

---

[43] Although as for my evidence on that I may be relying on Blackadder episodes as opposed to… you know… any actual history. I'll look it up later. I promise.

the opening of the chapter before I go on to talk about the Witch Trials in Elizabethan England.

My actual intention, by linking these events to the witch trials, was twofold. Firstly to make us think about the witch trials when we begin to look at things such as the response to terrorism in the world today, and keeping a measured response – and indeed in avoiding scapegoating in general. There is, however, a more important point, which is that I want those things to be in the back of your mind when I talk about the witch trials.

If I made a joke about the Holocaust or 9/11 in this book, I would think about it very carefully and make sure that I could justify it. If I make a joke about the First World War, I will think about it very carefully, even a flippant comment I would go over and over, trying to decide whether I can include it in this book. The burning of Catholics in Elizabethan England, however, I am happy to make an offhand, flippant comment about with no qualms, and I will happily make light-heat hearted comments amidst the deeper points about many darker historic events, and this troubles me a little.

If you meet me in the real world, and get into my close circle of friends, I will make inappropriate jokes or silly comments about tragic events – humour is part of the way I cope with tragedy in my life and in the world – but I would not make these comments in print, or in a public forum, because causing offence is not my aim in my work. I feel on safe ground making these comments about Elizabethan Witch Trials though – they are far enough removed in time that I am unlikely to cause offense through the jokes. I think it is Lenny Bruce who is often given credit for first summing this thought up as 'Comedy equals tragedy plus distance'[44], and in this case the distance is time.

Is this right though? Should I feel safer in this area? Should we feel more comfortable with jokes about people who died a long

---

[44] This is almost certainly misquoted, and it doesn't matter, because I have heard other people quoted as the originator of this phrase, I just chose the one I heard first.

time ago than about people who died a hundred years ago, or ten years ago, or last week? Let's get down to some facts about Elizabethan witchcraft while you have a little ponder about that.

In Elizabethan England there were 'witches' of a sort, and let's immediately separate out the 'fairy-tale' witch from the facts here. These witches were more often referred to as 'Wise Women', and most took on the role of healers in a time when medicine was very hit and miss anyway. These 'Wise Women' usually treated with medicines and ointments, the recipes for which had been passed down from mother to daughter by mouth, not written down, and some of them would have worked being based on knowledge of what the herbs did, and the results which had been achieved before.

Witches were, however, seen to be practitioners of magic, and many would offer charms to ward off evil spirits as well – this being a time when religion and beliefs in evil spirits prevailed, and with the bubonic plague returning every few generations and no real understanding of the causes of illness, people tended to reach around for scapegoats, as they continue to until this day, and blame came to rest on these women (usually) who were often slightly outside of society – often respected, but just as often the object of jealousy or fear for their position of respect.

With the invention of the printing press in the early-mid 1400s documents and books – and in the main religious texts – suddenly became available in far greater numbers than ever before in history, and ideas spread much faster, including ideas linking witchcraft to the Devil, and to the Black Death – then assumed by most people to be a punishment from God.

By 1562 Queen Elizabeth was forced to update the law against witchcraft, and with her government she did so in the Witchcraft Act, which made all forms of conjuring, enchantments and witchcraft (or "Conjuracions Inchauntmentes and Witchecraftes" as it was originally spelt) illegal, and paved the way for trials, and killing of witches. Not, however, torture and burning.

In creating the law Elizabeth did not, unlike in the rest of Europe, define witchcraft as heresy, but just declared it illegal instead. These days to many people in a multicultural and multi-faith world, where in most countries there is at least a degree of religious freedom, it may seem strange that arguing with established beliefs would carry more weight than other crimes of the time. In this period, however, a crime of heresy would have meant this was a religious and Church matter, and burnings and torture would have been deemed appropriate punishments. As it was without the involvement of heresy it was purely a state matter, and so the harshest sentence was hanging (not a good result, but a kinder death than burning) and lesser crimes could be punished by time in the stocks.

Elizabeth's reasons for not going to town on witchcraft in line with most of the rest of Europe are interesting in themselves. The first is that England was, under Elizabeth, still a Protestant nation, and most of Europe was following pronouncements from the Pope that witchcraft was the work of Satan, and therefore heresy by default. Far more interestingly, however, is the suggestion that Elizabeth herself may have had some involvement with witchcraft, or certainly elements which could be considered witchcraft to the people of the time.

Anne Boleyn, Elizabeth's mother, was accused of being a witch, although there are debates about how far these allegations went, and to what extent they played any role in her execution following her divorce from Henry VIII. The possible allegations stem mainly from the fact that she apparently had a mole or birthmark on her chin, and a sixth finger growing from her little finger – which were clear signs that her enemies could point to as evidence when slandering her. Although there is no actual evidence that Boleyn ever had actual involvement in witchcraft, there is the possibility that if Elizabeth knew of the rumours that this may be a reason why she went 'softly' when creating the law[45].

Enough about the actual law that was created, now to bring us back to the angle I wanted to take on this at the start of the

---

[45] And once again I point out that 'softly' in this case means hanging rather than being burned at the state, so it is a very relative term.

chapter and to consider how these laws, created out of irrational fear and prejudice, were put into effect.

Bear in mind that some of those people who were found guilty of these crimes were guilty – some of them practised witchcraft and believed themselves to be capable of cursing other people, and had deliberately done so. For these people it wasn't a mental health issue, these people were not insane, they were people who believed the same as the majority of people in society – just they actually wanted and were prepared to do evil deeds through their beliefs. So even though their actions would not kill by magic, there was intent there, and they believed as much as their accusers that they were guilty of at least 'attempted' murder. I make this point just because it is easy to think of all people accused of witchcraft as innocent, because they weren't really casting spells, but I think that intent matters in this situation. It is fair to suggest, however, that the majority were guilty of nothing more than practicing a particular set of prohibited beliefs, and others innocent even of this.

So finally some numbers, and these are the best numbers I can find – I apologise now if you find a different set of numbers. I have found a couple, but they are relatively close. I won't live and die by these numbers though – even if you offer me hanging instead of burning at the stake.

Of two-hundred and seventy Elizabethan Witch Trials, only twenty-three were men, not even ten per cent of the total, and of the women the vast majority were single, older women. Of course class was a big issue back then – and guess which class in society the majority of those accused came from. The poor, of course. The people who were accused, and when found guilty either pilloried or executed - in Essex alone between 1560 and 1603 fifty-eight people were hung under the Elizabethan Witchcraft Act – were clearly from a section in society where they had little defence or protection, and made easy scapegoats.

This brings us full circle back to the start of this chapter, and my links to more modern attempts to scapegoat and cast out people – even to extremes of violence and genocide today, and why it is important we remember it. I heard someone talking the other day about 'foreign workers coming over and taking our jobs'[46] . I'm sure you've heard something similar. Or sat on a train and see somebody wince, become alert, or stare just a little too long at the Muslim student who has got on with his backpack full of textbooks.

It is for every person to be vigilant – not watching out for the next perceived threat from within the country, the next group of people who are going to threaten us. Rather for us each to watch ourselves and make sure we can't be seen as guilty of scapegoating, spreading blame, or targeting a group of innocent people, however we define them. If we aren't careful we will find ourselves guilty of starting another witch hunt, and the 20th Century version of that was the Holocaust. I dread to think what the 21st Century version could be.

---

[46] Yes, they did give a specific nationality, and I'm not going to be specific here, because it isn't important.

Music Hall and Variety
The Good Old Days?

I have been asked a number of times whether I would prefer to live in the past, in a number of different situations. The first, and most common, is when I express displeasure with technology – which I confess to doing a lot more than is fair. What I hate most about technology is the way I get caught up with it. I was probably in the last year to go through school to Sixth Form where we just didn't have mobile phones in schools. Maybe there were a couple by the time we reached Sixth Form, but generally telephones were in houses, and smartphones were not even imagined. When I entered senior school I remember being amazed that there were a couple of computers in the school library which actually had the internet – incredible![47]

So I moan that the internet stops people going to libraries, or that the iPhone is far too much when all I want is a phone, but that doesn't stop me looking up the odd fact on the internet when I can't get to the library, and I have wasted a lot of my life playing Temple Run on my iPhone. I won't, however, upgrade to the newest iPhone unless this one breaks, and even then I'll get whatever they will send me free on my contract – but I probably wouldn't downgrade. So while I am not a fan of technology, it has wormed its way into my life. So I don't think I would cope well going back a couple of hundred years to before there were even the first telephones.

Then there is transport. I have a thing for steam trains, and I've been lucky over the last year to be involved with some writing and performance work at the Isle of Wight Steam Railway which has given me plenty of opportunities to take journeys along their track

---

[47] And it is a mark of how quickly technology is corrupted that I know that all the pornography sites were blocked. Not that I would have looked myself of course – in year 7 I was far too good for that!

in some of their carriages. I often feel sad that the world has been so shrunk by flight, and would love to shun modern air travel in favour of going everywhere by ground where it is possible. On the other hand I do a lot of work in Italy, and I need to be able to get there in a day so that I can book work up to the day I leave, or on the day after (or sometimes the evening of) my return. Without aeroplanes this would be impossible, and so travelling back in time before this would be troublesome.

That is before I attempt to find a time in the past to travel to, where I would be unlikely to die of plague, or sent off to war, or in other ways to die very young.

Overall I am happy to be living today and just studying the past, but if there is one thing I regret about not having been born at a different period in history it is that these days we are in the world of television and film, and in a world where live performance, and particularly variety performances, are the exception rather than the rule for most people.

A couple of days ago I went to the Thursford Christmas Spectacular up in Norfolk. It is an event my parents have been telling me about for years, but this is the first time my tour schedule allowed me to make it to watch the show, and it was an amazing experience – well deserving of the name 'Spectacular'. I don't want this chapter to descend into a review of the show, that isn't the point, but it was a variety performance with over a hundred performers, including singers, dancers, an orchestra, juggler, comedian and bagpipes. It is the sort of performance you don't get to see so much of anymore, and yet it plays to packed out audiences and the whole audience seemed to enjoy it as much as I did. Even in this performance, however, the actual range of variety was small, focusing on the singers and dancers.

If anything could tempt me back to the past it would be life in the heydays of Music Hall and Variety Theatre, where singers, dancers, comedy performers and speciality acts were the main forms of entertainment. Like pantomime, Music Hall was quite specific to England, although other countries had similar things, such as vaudeville in the States.

In fact at this point I'm going to go off on a brief digression to talk about pantomime, because there will be people reading this (at least I certainly hope that someone will be reading this) in America and much of Europe who think that I am being a bit Anglo centric in saying that pantomime is a British thing. I have faced this problem before, because in other countries when they say pantomime, we in England would call it just 'mime'. They mean the acting without talking – you know, walking into the wind and all the other things which I never quite got right when I studied at the Physical Theatre Studio in Turin. In Britain, however, pantomime is different.

I was actually in Tennessee in 2005 when I got my first professional performing job, in a pantomime touring in Wales, and I was keen to tell everyone. This led to much hilarity when I tried to explain what seemed simple to me. At Christmas we have a type of show usually based around a famous fairy tale so that everybody already knows the story. Not only the story, but everybody also already knows most of the jokes, and how they are supposed to react to some of them. The lead boy is usually played by a girl in a costume that shows a lot of leg, while one of the lead women, the 'Dame' is always played by a man. Oh, and it's a family show. Is that so hard to understand? Oh, no it isn't!

Let's put the world of pantomime behind us and get back to the Music Halls. Although Music Hall entertainment was big from 1850 until it died out around 1960, when television began its assault on live performance, the peak in popularity and the height of the Music Halls in Britain was really between about 1870 and the end of the First World War.

The early Music Halls began in venues not unlike a lot of fringe theatre venues in London today, in taverns and public houses. Much like performing any sort of act in a pub, or beer festival today, the performers would have had to work to get the attention of the audiences, who would be there for a drink and a chat as well as to take in the entertainment – I know, I've been there. Also, like a sort of heckler from hell in a comedy performance, the audiences would be perfectly prepared to hurl abuse at the performers, although unlike most places today they would often also throw anything that they could lay their hands on from bottles to, on one occasion, apparently, a dead cat.

As the popularity of the Music Hall style of entertainment grew, custom build Music Halls began to open, the first being the seven hundred seat Canterbury Hall in Lambeth in 1852, the owner of which even introduced the idea of letting women into the audience. It was the first of many, and in 1870, according to one statistic, there were thirty-one large halls serving the people of London, and a further three hundred and eighty-five spread out across the towns and cities in the rest of the country, and the performers were stars. According to the Victoria and Albert Museum, by 1875 there were three hundred and seventy-five in the Greater London area alone! This was a colossal number of venues, and gave work to a large number of performers. The money wasn't good, and the work was hard, but I have never met a performer who would complain about hard work and little money in return for the chance to perform a lot in good venues.

Don't get me wrong, there is work for live performers these days, just not on quite the same level as there was back in the heyday of Music Hall. In that period performers of all types could perform in several of the London halls every night, in between touring the provinces. I have spent a lot of time touring shows, and while touring schools in Italy I frequently played two schools in a day. However this doesn't even begin to compare with the idea of playing several London Music Halls in an evening.

It was in this period that the Music Halls often became bigger and moved into buildings built or restyled to borrow more from theatre stage design, and moved into the era where Music Hall blends with Variety theatre.

These days the majority of my variety work, in the form of my escapology, is performed at arena events such as Steam or Village Shows, where a series of variety acts are booked as part of a larger event. People gather around the arena to watch my escapes, or a strongwoman act, a tightrope walker or other variety acts all trying to keep different performance arts alive, and live, in an era of television, and especially of reality television.

These, like the performers in the Music Halls, are people who have honed their acts and worked hard, and they are generally rewarded by an audience that enjoys it. Live performance has, however, become the exception rather than the rule, and when it is seen it is musicals that get the majority of the audiences. Again it is because of television. Most variety acts don't work so well on television, because you lose the thrill of a live performance. A musical, however, can work in a film. It can feature stars off the television, household names that everybody knows from the friendly box in the corner of the room[48].

For me a world where live performances were more common, and variety acts were more prominent would appeal immediately if I found myself a time machine. This wouldn't even be a selfish thing about wanting there to be more work and glory for me – it would be selfish in that I would want to be able to see more of the great variety performers performing locally all the time. Maybe I'm just old fashioned, obviously television is here to stay, but I think there is still room for live variety and Music Hall style performances in this world, and I for one hope that I don't have to travel back in time to see a bit more of a comeback.

---

[48] Ok, I'm probably living in the past even here. I mean a television, obviously, even though chances are yours is practically flat and hanging on the wall.

1066

Because I felt I had to.

I spent a lot of time trying to decide whether or not to include this subject in the book. I have started writing it a few times, then decided not to include it, and then deleted it. A little bit later on I feel a bit guilty about leaving out the only date a lot of people know in English history - although 'date' might be a little generous as it is a year, not exactly a date!

This for me seemed to be a double-edged sword; people would recognise the date and may expect it to be found in any collection of histories from England. Because it is so often included, however, this means that it is also a subject that has been written about many times, and included in countless books, films and comedy sketches, and so I felt that maybe I would just be repeating things.

I went through the same process a couple of years ago when I was writing my one man show about the History of Britain, and in that situation I got around it by presenting the Battle of Hastings through the medium of interpretive dance... one of my personal favourite physical comedy moments in the show (and one which seems to go down well with audiences as well).

It strikes me at this point that I have made a big assumption in the opening of the chapter, and in making this assumption I have supported my point. I have assumed that when you hear ten-sixty-six you immediately thought of the Battle of Hastings, even if you weren't entirely sure exactly what the battle was and who it was between. I would imagine that the majority of people probably also thought William the Conqueror, arrow in the eye, or The Bayeux Tapestry[49].

---

[49] Although I'm really only referring to English people here. I'm not sure

If you didn't immediately think any of these things then don't worry. If you did I hope you will still find the chapter interesting as it reminds you of some of the things you have long since forgotten, and hopefully bringing up some fun facts about the battle that you may not have been aware of.

Like the Hundred Years War, the Battle of Hastings and the Norman Conquest of England came down to arguments over who the rightful King of England was, this time following the death of Edward The Confessor in January 1066. It is possible that Edward may have been partially to blame for the confusion. He died without having fathered any children, and so there were no direct heirs, but according to some Norman sources Edward had promised the crown to William. William would later become famous to us as William the Conqueror, but at this point was referred to by the less kind title of William the Bastard, although, one imagines, not to his face. This was owing to the fact that he was the illegitimate son of the Duke of Normandy, rather than being a slight on his personality.

To add a spark of interest, the news that Edward had declared William as his successor was apparently delivered by Harold Godwinson, who promised to support William's claim to the throne. Until, on Edward's deathbed, the old King apparently changed his mind and declared that Harold would be his successor instead, and Harold decided he would rather support his own claim to the throne, and took the crown for himself.

This somewhat annoyed William, to say the least, and so on 27th September 1066 he set sail to England with his army to resolve the question of the succession in the time honoured manner, war.

This was bad timing for Harold, who had been busy in York fighting off an invasion force of Vikings on the 25th, and on the 1st October got word that William's army had occupied Hastings, requiring Harold to march his tired army back down the country to Senlac Hill in Battle, East Sussex. This is where the battle would be

---

how important this element of English history would be to the rest of the world!

fought, not Hastings itself. It was a conveniently named place for a battle - although I would be willing to concede the possibility that it was named later as a result of the battle.

Threats and attempts at negotiations were arranged, but eventually on 14th October 1066 the Battle of Hastings took place, beginning with a somewhat unlikely first casualty.

Taillefer is apparently the name of the first man killed in the Battle of Hastings, and his position on the front line was not as a warrior, a knight, or even an over ambitious squire. He was, in fact, a jester, and therefore has my respect and sympathy for his profession. That day he began his act in the usual way, a bit of singing and sword juggling. At the end of his act, however, he suddenly decided there may be a better use for the sword, and decided to attack the shield wall of Harold's army. Such an attack was never going to be a recipe for success, and he was quickly dispatched before the real fighting got underway.

From here on in things get pretty confusing. To fully understand any battle is difficult, and to understand a battle in hindsight using a tapestry as one of your main sources of evidence is even more so, but we can pretty much give a summary of the battle as follows.

The fight begins with the Norman army attacking, and this began hours of intense fighting - at some point during which the Norman archers decide instead of firing directly at Harold's men to instead fire upwards raining arrows down on them. This lost a lot of English men their eyes, and one of the arrows struck Harold just above the right eye, wounding him.

It is then that the Normans carry out a masterpiece of strategic battle, when they retreat. Harold's army lose discipline in the excitement of seeming victory, and break ranks to pursue the fleeing Normans, only to find that it was a feint, and with the English ranks already broken the Norman knights on horseback can make short work of destroying the army.

At some point during this – the how and who are open to a lot of discussion – the wounded Harold is killed by four Knights, one of whom may have been William himself, and he is dismembered. By Christmas day of 1066 William had put down the last of the enemy troops, and was crowned at Westminster Abbey.

William ruled England mostly from France, but he suffered his own humiliation after his death. As he was being buried his body was slightly too large for the space in the tomb in which it was being interred, and it burst. As if this wasn't bad enough for the body of a King, in 1562 his bones were taken during the French Wars of Religion, and all but a thigh bone were lost. This is all that is now buried in the tomb of William the Conqueror.

It is funny how dates can be important. Most English people know the date of 1066 as the last time England was invaded by a foreign power – carefully forgetting that Edward the Confessor himself was already half Norman, and that, as there was no other great overthrow of power, the 'foreign invaders' which are referred to crop up in the ancestry of most English people today.

Most actual information about the battle is forgotten, but people speak proudly of the fact that England has not been invaded since that time –which for me shows a typical English view of things. We don't remember the dates of every battle that England has won over the centuries. No, the date we remember is the last time we had a battle for our country on our shores, and we lost.

The British Empire
Why I feel better about it in Italy than in England

These days, it appears, we British aren't supposed to feel proud of our Empire[50]. In fact for a long time there seems to have been a feeling of guilt, of trying to brush it under the carpet, instead of pride.

Personally I could live with feeling neither; I wasn't actually part of the British Empire at all, having been born a long time after the empire had dwindled away from the time when the 'sun never set', to now, when the empire consists of a few islands here and there, and isn't even referred to as an empire anymore. So I could make a logical argument, as many do, that I have no right to either pride or guilt for the fact that I happened to be born in this country.

I can't, however, change the fact that I am English and British, and proud of being both, however irrational that may be. I am proud of all the good things that our country has done over the centuries, and as a result it is only fair that I should allow some sadness, if not direct guilt, for the things that the nation has done wrong. In the case of our Empire, however grand and expansive it was, and however many benefits it gave to people around the world, there can be no denying that it also involved the invasion and conquest of indigenous people. It involved killing, and until 1807 there was a strong slave trade – with slavery itself not outlawed throughout the Empire until 1833.

---

[50] I know, I know. Earlier I made a big thing about the English Civil War, and this being a book about English history, and now I'm talking about the 'British Empire'. Well guess what – it's my book, and I will make and change the rules as it suits me to do so. I have something to write about this subject, and so the rules are being changed!

This is one of the reasons I have enjoyed spending a lot of time in Italy over the past few years. There are few nations in the world that can come close to claiming something similar to the British Empire. The USA may be the biggest superpower in the world today, but it is not an empire with control over the world, however much some presidents, security services and even, sadly people outside the USA - including glove-puppet Blair - seem to think it is.

In the days of colonies there were other countries with overseas interests, other nations as involved in slavery as Britain, but none of these had Empires the size or power of the British. I'm sure people will come up with other Empires which were large, but the British Empire covered about a third of the world's population at its height, and about a quarter of the land surface of the world. It was pretty impressive in scale, however you feel about the morality.

I think that in history there has only been one empire with the might, size, and historical weight to equal the British Empire, and that is the Roman Empire. Sure the Roman Empire didn't cover as much of the total Earth's surface as the British Empire, but it covered a huge percentage of the 'known world' at that time. Both Empires had remarkable similarities in both their bad points, and some of their saving graces.

I mentioned this to someone in Italy not so long ago, and they got a little bit uptight.

"The Roman Empire", they told me, "was good and progressive and made life better for the people and drove progress forwards. The British Empire was evil and destroyed other cultures."

At least they said something like that – my Italian is good, but I'm probably paraphrasing a little. This made me think for a minute – after I took the time to point out that as her family is from Turin, that they were invaded by the Romans as much as the British were, even though a lot of people now seem to think of Roman and Italian as synonymous in history. That, however, is a discussion for another book.

The fact is that there is this double standard when thinking about the Roman and British Empires, and it is a double standard of time. We apportion blame to the British Empire as though we expect it to have behaved better, while we forgive a lot of the Roman Empire's shortcomings as 'progress'.

I'm not going to go down the Monty Python route of questioning what the Romans ever did for us[51]. They did bring progress in some areas, although not as much as people think. In the time before Romans invaded Britain there were already roads – despite the fact that people often talk about the Roman's creating and inventing roads. The pre-Roman roads were often made with wood, and there are examples surviving today. The Romans brought a different style of roads, and a standard style of roads, but they did not bring 'roads'.

Of course Romans brought some 'progress' and advancements in technology to Britain, and my point here isn't to say that they didn't. It is to make the point that their technology was built on top of the native way of doing things. The Romans were not asked to come and bring their progress; theirs was an Empire of invasion and force. They would form relationships and enter countries and regions through negotiation if they could, but if not would expand through the might of their arms.

The British Empire also brought technological progress to many colonies throughout the world, from when tribes were first met and trading occurred, to areas where Britain set up full rule. In many areas the British Empire tried to negotiate their way into power in certain areas. In India, for example, when the rule moved from the private rule of the East India Trading Company to the government of Britain, the Indian princes and large land holders in the country were recognised and left in power, under the British of course, in return for not rebelling against British rule, in much the same way that the Romans would, as with their allegiance with Prasutagus[52].

---

[51] In case you haven't seen The Life Of Brian - the sanitation, the medicine, education, wine, public order, irrigation, roads, a fresh water system, and public health. Now go and watch the film.

Again I must point out that I am not saying that there is any way that this form of control is justified – I am not arguing an absolute moral point in this chapter at all. I'm just saying that the Roman and British Empires cannot be seen as different in the amount of good or ill that they have done in the world, or did when they were in power.

One of the most reprehensible crimes that I think the British Empire was guilty of is the destruction of other cultures and religions, and the attempt to 'civilise' places around the Empire, through the sending of missionaries and forcing the Christian religion onto native people, along with British ideas of decency. There are entire cultures that have been lost because of the British Empire's treatment of people in many of their colonies as 'lesser people', including, in the worst case the treatment of people as slaves, and the British involvement in setting up the slave trade.

These, obviously, are not things that I am going to attempt to defend the British Empire for. I have heard it said that the British Empire deserves some credit for abolishing the slave trade and eventually making slavery illegal, and there is some credit for this. The abolishment of the slave trade, however, does not in any way mitigate the fact that people from all over the world were taken from their homes and forced to travel to countries they had never seen to serve as slaves. In the same way that the Roman Armies would capture slaves from territories across the world and return them to Rome to serve there, as well as in other territories across the Empire, sometimes being forced into a life (and death) as gladiators in the arenas.

When it comes to the attacks on religions, and particularly smaller local religions, the British Empire and the missionaries who went out into tribes and countries as part of the Empire to spread their religion, and to put down other religions, are certainly guilty. There is no question that the Romans were also guilty of the suppression of religions and the spread of their own religions, in two waves – first spreading the Roman gods around the world and

---

[52] Remember? The husband of Boudicca from the first chapter? Bet you weren't expecting a last minute test that you were paying attention.]

claiming local gods for their own, or as versions of the Roman gods themselves. They then spread Christianity itself when that became the official religion of the Roman Empire.

All of this is simply to make the point that whether you consider the consequences of the British Empire as a good or evil thing, and whether you want to feel pride or guilt in the Empire if you are British, there is no getting over the fact that the same moral standards should be applied to the Roman Empire. We cannot see the Romans as beacons of enlightenment while we see the British Empire as evil and bad, we must accept that both Empires had elements of bringing progress, and elements which were morally unjustifiable.

That is why I feel better about the British Empire when I am Italy than anywhere else in the world. As far as I see it the Italians tend to claim the Roman Empire as much as I have any claim to the British Empire. Other countries I visit may have been harmed by the British Empire, or at least be neutral to it. When I am in Italy, however, I am the one who comes from a country which was overrun by the other's Empire in the past. I feel nothing in terms of annoyance over that, and do not think they have any reason to feel guilt for it. It does, however, give me the opportunity to put the guilt I feel over the British Empire to one side for a while, and think about its achievements.

For those people who think that there is no order in what I write, that maybe I just choose a subject that interests me, do some research, and then ramble on about it for a few pages, this chapter, the last historical subject I cover in this book, will prove ever so slightly that I do think ahead on occasion. In this chapter I have cunningly linked English History through the British Empire to the Roman Empire, and therefore Italian History. As mentioned I have spent a lot of time in Italy and come to think of is as a sort of second home, and so now I finish this book, and I will begin my new task, investigating the history of Italy, and trying to find some interesting subjects for the next volume of Condensed Histories.

Final Thoughts
Why dig up the past?

I bet that at the end of that chapter you thought you were rid of me, right. Well, I found something else to say before I go off to work on the next one of these books.

A friend of mine put a status up on facebook the other day saying something along the lines of:

"Don't worry about the past; the present and future are what are important".

Reading this status really worried me, until I realised that they were probably referring to the fact that they had just been dumped or something, rather than making a statement against history books. Even though I knew that this was what she meant, the status still niggled at me, and I got to really thinking about it.

I have spent much of the two months pouring over history books, trying to decide what subjects I wanted to include in this book, studying far more about each subject than I would ever be able to use in a 'Condensed History', and basically living much of the time with my mind firmly in the past, sometimes the fairly distant past.

Instead of heading down to the pub to see if there were any women there who wanted to look at me with a combination of bewilderment and pity as I tried to chat them up, I spent evenings with Boudicca and her rebellion. Instead of heading up to Essex for a few days to spend time with my mates drinking and displaying all the principles of confirmation bias as we chat about those women with whom we have had success, or more commonly mock each other over those times we were less successful. Instead I spent time trying to decide whether I thought Seahenge should have been moved or not.

I have been, to all intents and purposes, wrapped up with the past more than I was the present - the first time I have been in that situation for any extended length of time since I finished my degree, and I really enjoyed getting back into it. As soon as this book is done and dusted I will begin preparation work on the next one so that I can keep my focus on the past.

The trouble was, that after I saw my friend's status I began to wonder whether she was right in the point which she wasn't actually making, if you follow me. Was she right that what is past is essentially done with, and that I ought to be focussed on the present instead of spending my time studying and writing about history, so that other people can then spend their time reading what I have written about the past. I began, essentially, to wonder what the point really is in history – a dangerous thing to do while working on a history book.

I hope in this book that I have achieved my primary aim of making history interesting, but also of showing how history can be linked to today. That the lessons of history are all around us, and whether they help make us better people, entertain us, or just occasionally make us think, I feel confident that there is a place for the past in this world. So rather than saying that the past is not important, I put it to you that we should follow the words of (in my opinion) the greatest of English writers, Mr Charles Dickens in his A Christmas Carol:

"I shall live in the Past, the Present, and the Future. The Spirits of all Three shall strive within me. I will not shut out the lessons that they teach!"

I really hope you have enjoyed reading this book as much as I have enjoyed writing it. If you have, or you want to correct any horrendous mistakes in the book, or argue with any of my thoughts on history, or let me know something I could cover in a future book or podcast, then let me know in one of the modern ways – send me a 'tweet' at @condensedhist. Or contact me through my website at www.condensedhistories.com, and while you're there check out my new Condensed Histories podcast.

For now let me extend my heartfelt thanks for staying with me on this little journey though some Condensed Histories, it has been a pleasure writing this book for you, and I hope to 'see' you again!

Greg

Greg Chapman

Isle of Wight

January 2013